MAKING PROGRESS

MAKING PROGRESS

Programmatic and Administrative Approaches for Multimodal Curricular Transformation

LOGAN BEARDEN

UTAH STATE UNIVERSITY PRESS
Logan

Published by Utah State University Press
An imprint of University Press of Colorado
245 Century Circle, Suite 202
Louisville, Colorado 80027

 The University Press of Colorado is a proud member of
the Association of University Presses.

The University Press of Colorado is a cooperative publishing enterprise supported, in part, by Adams State University, Colorado State University, Fort Lewis College, Metropolitan State University of Denver, Regis University, University of Alaska, University of Colorado, University of Denver, University of Northern Colorado, University of Wyoming, Utah State University, and Western Colorado University.

∞ This paper meets the requirements of the ANSI/NISO Z39.48–1992 (Permanence of Paper)

ISBN: 978-1-64642-212-8 (paperback)
ISBN: 978-1-64642-213-5 (ebook)
https://doi.org/10.7330/9781646422135

Library of Congress Cataloging-in-Publication Data

Names: Bearden, Logan, author.
Title: Making progress : programmatic and administrative approaches for multimodal curricular transformation / Logan Bearden.
Description: Logan : Utah State University Press, [2022] | Includes bibliographical references and index.
Identifiers: LCCN 2021050442 (print) | LCCN 2021050443 (ebook) | ISBN 9781646422128 (paperback) | ISBN 9781646422135 (ebook)
Subjects: LCSH: English language—Rhetoric—Study and teaching (Higher)—United States. | Media programs (Education)—United States. | Curriculum change—United States. | Academic writing—Curricula. | Modality (Linguistics) | Education, Higher—United States—Computer-assisted instruction. | English language—Rhetoric—Curricula—United States.
Classification: LCC PE1405.U6 B43 2022 (print) | LCC PE1405.U6 (ebook) | DDC 808/.0420711—dc23/eng/20211122
LC record available at https://lccn.loc.gov/2021050442
LC ebook record available at https://lccn.loc.gov/2021050443

The University Press of Colorado gratefully acknowledges Eastern Michigan University who supported, in part, this publication.

Cover illustration © MJgraphics/Shutterstock

To Nick: you're simply the best.

CONTENTS

ACKNOWLEDGMENTS

There are several expressions of gratitude that I must make because this book would never have been without the assistance of several organizations and individuals.

Thanks to the Department of English Language and Literature at Eastern Michigan University for offering me a research award that allowed me to fund research assistants, and many thanks to Joe Montgomery, Meg Phelps, Laura Kovick, and Briane Radke for their expert assistance in the process of coding and analyzing the data. To that end, I want to thank the Office of Research and Development at Eastern Michigan University, which provided multiphased support, funding everything from the earliest stages of data collection to the final stages of writing this manuscript.

A huge thank you goes to Derek Mueller, Chalice Randazzo, and Rachel Gramer, who are excellent colleagues and friends for providing their thoughtful feedback during all phases of the writing process.

Not least, this project would not have come to fruition without the ten composition program directors who so generously lent their expertise in the form of interviews. I am beyond thankful that they took the time to answer my questions (over the summer, no less!), and I consider myself blessed to be part of a discipline that includes such wonderful people who are doing innovative and exciting administrative and programmatic work.

MAKING PROGRESS

1

CARVING OUT SPACE FOR MULTIMODAL CURRICULAR TRANSFORMATION

"To ensure that our courses do not become irrelevant—or depending on one's perspective, to ensure that they do not become increasingly irrelevant—we must ask students to examine the designs of words on a page as well as the relationships among words, images, codes, textures, sounds, colors, and potentials for movement. We need, in short, to embrace composition" (Shipka, 2013, p. 211, emphasis added).

"Even though some scholars in the field have persuasively argued for the value of multimodal composing practices and the learning that occurs in the process, implementation of multimodal instruction has remained nominal in many writing programs. Attempts at implementing multimodal approaches are sporadic at best. Even those attempts are mostly individual instructors' initiatives in a handful of institutions. Multimodality—so highly hailed in scholarship as the means of preparing the writers and communicators of the future—is largely ignored in most writing classrooms. Frankly speaking, multimodality is still far from being a norm in the majority of writing classes, and it is miles away from being adopted by a large section of writing instructors and programs" (Khadka & Lee, 2019, p. 4).

Over the last 30 years, prominent scholars in writing studies have made persuasive and compelling arguments to expand the curricular circumference of composition, specifically first-year composition (FYC). In the introduction to their recent edited collection, Santosh Khadka and J. C. Lee (2019) list some of the major figures in the field who have made such calls: Cynthia Selfe, Kathleen Blake Yancey, Stuart Selber, Anne Wysocki, Geoffrey Sirc, and Jody Shipka, just to name a few (p. 3). Cynthia Selfe, for example, argued in 1999 about the "perils" the humanities face by not considering the ways in which digital technologies impact literate

https://doi.org/10.7330/9781646422135.c001

practices. Ten years later, in 2009, she went on to argue that "when we insist on print as the primary, and formally most acceptable, modality for composing knowledge, we . . . unwittingly limit students' sense of rhetorical agency" (p. 618). To teach alphabetic writing *only*, Selfe and these other figures argue, is to limit the rhetorical potentials of our students, especially in an increasingly digital world, where communicating with more than just words on a page is necessary.

As a discipline, those of us in writing studies have turned to the concept of *multimodality* and multimodal theory as a way to develop a more capacious composition curriculum. First, I would like to clarify what I mean when I invoke the term "multimodality," specifically the literate practices that the term describes and the value of a multimodal composition curriculum, because according to Pegeen Reichert Powell (2020), "perhaps the most persistent assumption about multimodality is that we know what it is" (p. 5). Multimodality, as a term, concept, and theory, comes from the study of linguistics and semiotics. Gunther Kress (2010) and others in the New London Group (NLG), have used the proliferation of digital technologies in the past 30 years to make the claim that there is a need to develop new pedagogies and curricula to prepare students to participate in the global-digital world by expanding the means of communication in which students are educated (Cope & Kalantzis, 2000). *Modes* are the building blocks of multimodal theory, and Kress defines a mode as a socially situated resource for communicating and lists image, writing, speech, music, gesture, and color as examples of modes (p. 1). Each of these have different affordances, different grammars, and different ways of communicating meaning, which are shaped by both the histories of their materialities and the social value of those materialities. For example, in print, alphabetic English, we read typed/graphic texts top to bottom, left to right, in (mostly) sequential order. Conversely, according to Kress (2005), images present all semiotic material at once, and he argues that this allows the audience of the image to follow points of individual interest: "It is the viewer's action that orders the simultaneously present elements in relation to her or his interest" (p. 13). Elsewhere, he claims that "in a social semiotic approach to mode, equal emphasis is placed on the affordance of the material 'stuff' of the mode (sound, movement, light, and tracing on surfaces, etc.) and on the work done with that material over very long periods" (2010, p. 80). In this way, he accounts for the ways in which we as meaning-makers shape the materials that make communication possible as much as our communications are influenced by the materials that we use. Indeed, per Kress, multimodality is a social-semiotic theory of communication that considers the symbiotic relationships among the contexts in which meaning-making takes place, the agents involved in the process, and not least, the semiotic potentials of the resources those agents employ. Although this theory describes a complex constellation, Paul Prior (2009) quite succinctly states that multimodality is a "routine dimension of language in use" (p. 16). In other words, communication and meaning-making are and always have been multimodal because multimodality is a central facet of literacy. Therefore, multimodality is not new; our (scholarly) attention to this phenomenon is new. This is the richness of multimodal theory: it emphasizes the materiality of communication and meaning-making, and it gives us a vocabulary with which we can theorize those processes. This is also why I choose to invoke the term "multimodal" rather than digital/new media, digital humanities, or digital rhetoric, because those terms allude to or imply the digital in ways that multimodal does not.

Multimodality—as a term and concept—has the ability to create more capacious composition programs by not prescribing the materials and media with/in which students work, thereby expanding their rhetorical potentials. Within this framework, alphabetic writing is but one in a capacious repertoire of skills necessary for communicating, which destabilizes the privileged position of print literacy, both in and out of the academy. Rather than theorizing the process(es) of writing only, a composition curriculum that attends to multimodality, as Bill Cope and Mary Kalantzis (2000) argue, "focuses on modes of representation much broader than language alone" (p. 5). These authors claim that "the changing world and the new demands being placed upon people as meaning makers in changing workplaces, as citizens in changing public spaces" (p. 4) outside of the academy demand transformed curricula within. In these revised programs and curricula, students learn about the role of design in literacy and meaning-making, utilize their personal, individual literacy practices through situated practice, and eventually exhibit transformed practice, which "involves students' transfer, reformulation, and redesign of existing texts and meaning-making practice from one context to another" (Angay-Crowder et al., 2013, p. 38). Students write in these programs, but they do not just write; they compose with/in a variety of materials and for multiple audiences, which prepares them to do so in the future.

We have, to be sure, responded generously to calls to expand the curricular content of composition. Teacher-scholars in writing studies/rhetoric and composition have made space for video (see, for example, Sheppard, 2009; VanKooten, 2016; VanKooten & Berkley, 2016), audio

(Ceraso, 2014; Ceraso, 2018; McKee, 2006), and design as a multimodal-rhetorical process (George, 2002; Hocks, 2003; Stroupe, 2000; Wysocki, 2005; Leverenz, 2014; Purdy, 2014). Further, we have a plethora of models of what these expanded, transformed curricula might look like, especially within individual classrooms (see Alvarez, 2016; Graban et al., 2013; Cope & Kalantzis, 2000; Cope & Kalantzis, 2009; Kynard, 2007; Martin et al., 2019; Rios, 2015; Shipka, 2013; Shipka, 2011). In "Made Not Only in Words," Kathleen Blake Yancey (2004a) details that transformed composition classes would emphasize an approach to rhetoric and literacy that acknowledges that "we *already* inhabit a model of communication practices incorporating multiple genres related to each other, those multiple genres remediated across contexts of time and space, linked one to the next, circulating across and around rhetorical situations both inside and outside of school. This is composition—*and* this is the *content* of composition" (p. 306, emphasis original). Indeed, the association of rhetoric with alphabetic writing only is a "by-product of print culture rather than the epistemological limits of rhetoric itself. We use rhetoric to help us think more clearly, write more elegantly, design more logically. . . . Rhetoric has always been important to the composition classroom, but we are only now beginning to understand how it might work as a device to help our students understand and create visually and verbally interwoven texts" (Handa, 2004, p. 2). Similarly, Joyce Walker (2007) has suggested that, in attending to a capacious understanding of rhetoric and literacy, these transformed curricula would "attend to the materiality of texts . . . [offering] students the opportunity to make knowledgeable choices about software, hardware, structural organization, and to examine the *rhetorical potentials of different visual, aural, and alphabetical compositions*" ("What does new media writing mean to you?" emphasis added). Thus, while the composition curriculum has traditionally encompassed rhetoric and literacy as they pertain to alphabetic writing, a multimodal composition curriculum expands the available means and materials of persuasion and communication, allowing students to cultivate a more nuanced understanding of their composing processes and choices. In doing so, the curriculum helps students become more effective composers both in and out of the academy.

These calls and arguments are persuasive, and the new curricula detailed in these publications are innovative and exciting. And yet, we see similar arguments appear again and again in our scholarship. In 2014, Carrie Leverenz wrote, "As a teacher concerned with my students' ability to participate in a future of writing, I believe we need to question our complicity with this predominantly conservative educational mission" of focusing on print, alphabetic writing as the sole content of composition (p. 2). This is a strikingly similar concern to the one Kathleen Blake Yancey raised in her 2004 Conference on College Composition and Communication Chair's Address, in which she demonstrated that "literacy today is in the midst of a tectonic change. Even inside of school, never before have writing and composing generated such diversity in definition. What do our references to writing mean? Do they mean print only?" (2004a, p. 298). Yancey's claim then—the urgency of which was made even more potent by the data she cited demonstrating alarming declines in enrollment in traditional English departments—was yet another iteration of Selfe's 1999 admonition about the perils of not paying attention. To put it plainly, leading scholars have urged *repeatedly* for us to make these curricular, programmatic changes, and we have a wealth of scholarship including models of those changes, but as Emily Isaacs (2018) has argued, "what is a trend in the literature and conversation at conferences is often revealed not to be the case when we look systematically" at individual institutions (p. 47). This is especially true of multimodal composition. In an article detailing an examination of composition textbooks, Aubrey Schiavone (2017) writes:

> Instruction in composition has tended to privilege the *production* of text and the *consumption* of visual and multimodal artifacts. In this way, my findings demonstrate a disparity between theories and practices associated with multimodal composing, especially at the juncture in composition's relationship with multimodality that these textbooks capture. *Theories* posit the importance of teaching students to produce visual and multimodal compositions, while the *practices* encapsulated in textbook prompts tend to promote the consumption of multimodal compositions more so than their production. (p. 359, emphasis added)

There persists a profound disconnect between the changes for which leading figures and key scholarship advocate and the day-to-day realities of composition programs, and that disconnect, as Jody Shipka outlines in the quote included at the beginning of this chapter, places the future of composition at risk.

To illustrate a possible explanation for this vexed issue, I offer a brief story of my personal experience with multimodal composition. Multimodality became a part of my pedagogy in my first semester of teaching FYC. Specifically, I included what Wendy Bishop (2002) called a "radical revision" as the final major project in ENC 1101: Freshman Composition and Rhetoric. In his description of Bishop's assignment, Jeff Sommers (2014) states that the radical revision asks students to "consider changes in voice/tone, syntax, genre, audience, time, physi-cal layout/typography, *or even medium*" (p. 295, emphasis added). In my course, I asked students to take one of the projects they had composed earlier in the semester—an academic essay four to seven pages in length about the students' digital literacy practices—and transform it into a different medium for a different audience. These requirements meant that the products were necessarily multimodal. The students made scrapbooks, posters, paintings, and videos, all of which required that they consider sounds, color, images, etc., and how those resources com-municate to nonacademic audiences. They had the final 2 weeks of the semester to complete the task, it was worth 10% of their final grades, and I cannot recall if we actually spent any time in class discussing draft-ing and revising such projects. They handed it in to me on the last day of class, and I never saw most of those students again. I do not know what the students learned from the project, or whether they found it to be a productive intellectual task, because I never bothered to ask them how it might have influenced their understanding of rhetoric and/or of the composing process.

The following year I taught a class called Writing about Harry Potter and Pop Culture, a theme-based FYC course that I designed to incorporate an early iteration of the teaching-for-transfer (TFT) cur-riculum developed by Liane Robertson and Kara Taczak.[1] The third major project in that class received a full month of time in the course schedule and was another variation of a radical revision: a multigenre, multimedia project that students used to share researched arguments composed in a previous assignment—an 8–10 page, double-spaced application of literary/cultural theory to the Harry Potter series—with audiences outside of the classroom. The students staged protests, created social media accounts, posted their fliers and posters around campus, were asked questions as they drew with chalk on the sidewalks between buildings, using multiple modes to convey their arguments and share their research. Alongside this assignment, students submit-ted a rationale that explained the rhetorical choices they made in their compositions and a reflection that explained what they learned about composing.

---

1. Kara Taczak and Liane Robertson were finishing their dissertation research projects as I began my graduate studies and teaching appointment at Florida State University. The pilot TFT curriculum that they utilized to collect their first rounds of data was detailed in FSU's Teacher's Guide, and I used that description to inform my own course. The results of those studies were shared in the 2014 book they co-authored with Kathleen Blake Yancey, *Writing Across Contexts*.

I *loved* that assignment for several reasons. First, while the low-stakes radical revision I assigned during my first semester was fairly stress-free for me and the students, I know that no one but me and the students ever saw those projects. The multigenre option that second year required that students circulate their work, sharing it with people who were not me. This reminded them that composing is inherently social, that people do interact with texts, that texts do work out in the world, and, not least, that texts beyond the academy require multimodal composing to reach their audience effectively. Second, those students were able to articulate to me what they had learned in reflection—they shared what it was like to have people interact with their online social media accounts or to have someone ask them about their research while they drew with sidewalk chalk—and explain *why* they created their compositions the way that they did. Those documents demonstrated specifically what and how those students learned about composition and rhetoric. Third, my colleagues began asking me about my classes after seeing student projects across campus and online. Those conversations provided me with an exigence, a kairotic opportunity, to discuss my values as an instructor of composition, to think through counter-arguments for the "how is this even writing?" question that plagues multimodal instruction, and to reflect on my teaching practices.

The multimodal assignment included in the Harry Potter class was better than the one I assigned in ENC1101. However, there was a major flaw with that project: *I made the decision to include it in my course.* The TFT curriculum I used to develop the assignment for the Harry Potter class was one of five or six options presented in the program guide, which came predesigned with weekly plans, assignment sheets, readings, activities, assessment rubrics, etc. so that instructors could select one, personalize the template information with their office location and email, and walk into class (somewhat) ready to deliver a curriculum on the first day. This particular assignment was *not* something to which the entire College Composition program was committed. Many composition programs in the country follow this model—crafting a fairly flexible curriculum from/with/in which instructors can make their own choices to align with programmatic goals. Multimodal composition, as a curricular component, can be taken up by those instructors and delivered to students. Or it cannot. Such flexibility, while certainly beneficial, does not allow for what is absolutely necessary: making sure that the entire program becomes committed to multimodal composition, delivering that commitment consistently to all students within the program, helping students become more adroit twenty-first-century composers in the process.

The programmatic restructuring that I am envisioning here is what Jason Palmeri (2012) has termed multimodal curricular transformation. While Palmeri does not offer a specific, concrete definition of this concept in his book, I will work toward one here. First, the choice of "curricular transformation" in Palmeri's term is worth noting because, according to Jennifer Grant Haworth and Clifton F. Conrad (1990), curricular transformation refers to "those informal and formal procedures through which knowledge within the curriculum is *continually* produced, created, and expanded by a wide range of stakeholders acting within a broader social and historical context" (p. 3, emphasis added). Similarly, Stephanie G. Hein and Carl D. Reigel (2011) argue that revision and transformation are different programmatic tasks because "curricular transformation does not stop at curricular revision," but rather, it "involves radical changes in structure, content, outcomes, *and at times, even culture*" (p. 3, emphasis added), which "requires continuous improvement efforts" (p. 8). Curricular transformation, then, is an ongoing process of programmatic remaking through reflective praxis, which has the potential to shift programmatic cultures, making space for new and different kinds of curricular content, like multimodal composition. Second, Palmeri suggests that a transformed multimodal composition curriculum would include the following features: (a) flexible ways for using multimodality as invention and revision techniques (p. 149), (b) engaging rhetorical concepts to compose multimodal texts (p. 152), and (c) providing students with the opportunity to use multimodal texts to cultivate critical digital literacies (p. 158). Based on these features, multimodal curricular transformation does not mean ancillary, low-stakes assignments tacked on to the end of the semester, which only work to reinforce the privileged position that print, alphabetic writing possesses within the academy (Whithaus, 2005; Alexander & Rhodes, 2014). Rather, multimodal curricular transformation describes a continual, intentional *infusion* of multimodality throughout the curriculum and a *redefinition of* the work of the composition classroom from alphabetic writing to rhetoric, including the full available means of persuasion and requiring that students utilize multimodal composition to demonstrate rhetorical proficiency. It is not the inclusion of flashier digital technologies in first-year composition courses; it is a call to craft programs that reflect what we know and believe about literacy and meaning-making and that foster the development of a capacious repertoire of rhetorical skills necessary for students to be more effective and engaged citizens. This is what we need to address the problems described above, and we must acknowledge that writing about multimodality in our scholarship and including it in our individual classrooms is not enough to lead to transformation. While a multimodal composition curriculum is delivered to students via instructors, it cannot be the sole responsibility of the individual instructor—those instructors graduate, retire, move to a different institution, etc., taking their innovative pedagogies and assignments with them when they go. It must be an ongoing program-wide commitment.

However, as I mentioned earlier in this chapter, we have not yet been able to accomplish this across programs at the national level. Khadka and Lee remind us in no uncertain terms that multimodal composition is *not* a common curricular component in FYC. There are many possible, interrelated reasons for this. First, too often, when those who are not familiar with multimodal theory and scholarship encounter the term "multimodal," they presume that it means "digital." When we conflate these, Jody Shipka (2013) suggests we "may severely limit the kinds of texts and communicative strategies or processes students explore in our courses" (p. 74). In short, Shipka suggests, when we prescribe "digital" (or any other kind of mode/medium for our students), we limit students' rhetorical possibilities: the texts they make, the audiences to whom they speak, and the spaces in which they can effect change. Similarly, we rarely present a consistent definition of multimodality to students. In a previous article, I isolated four types of multimodal outcomes: (a) multimodality as the simple addition of another mode on top of writing curricula (typically public speaking or discussion); (b) multimodality as visual rhetoric (prescribing that image be the mode through which students communicate); (c) multimodality as digital or technological literacy; and (d) multimodality as material-rhetorical flexibility, making use of the full available means of communication appropriate for the purpose and situation (Bearden, 2019a). Only the fourth category enacts a multimodal curriculum in the way that scholarship suggests it should.

Additionally, even if we do not conflate multimodality with digitality, multimodal composition can be met with resistance from the teaching faculty within the program. We know that instructors resist certain curricular changes if those changes challenge their personal construct or self-efficacy (Dryer, 2012; Ebest, 2005). These instructors may not understand how multimodality fits within the composition curriculum or are worried that they lack the technical/technological expertise necessary to make a multimodal curriculum work (Horn, 2002; Khalil, 2013; Moerschell, 2009; Oreg, 2006). It would make sense for instructors to resist a composition curriculum that diverges so greatly from their personal conception of first-year composition. Or these instructors might perceive multimodality (as it has been defined above) as a valuable part of composition curricula generally, but that it does not necessarily need to be something that students encounter in FYC. I disagree; multimodality is inextricable from composition (as a literate practice and field of study), and therefore *must* be situated within FYC. For years, scholarly conversations have engaged the question of FYC's curricular content. For example, Doug Downs and Elizabeth Wardle (2007), in their description of a reimagined version of FYC that functions as an introduction to writing studies, argue that the content should shift from "teaching 'academic writing' to *teaching realistic and useful conceptions of writing*" (p. 557). Rather than teaching students grammars or "absolute rules" associated with academic writing, this FYC introduces to students how writing actually functions, sharing disciplinary knowledge with them. One of the core threshold concepts of our discipline is that all writing is multimodal (Ball & Charlton, 2015), and, following Downs and Wardle's example, as one of the central principles of our discipline, *multimodality must be a part of FYC.* This does not mean that students leave our classes proficient in any one kind of multimodal composing (filmmaking/video, for example, could be explored in greater depth in an upper-level, major-specific course). This does mean, however, that multimodality is the purview of FYC: Students should understand that meaning-making is multimodal; students should begin to think about (if not theorize and practice) the limitations and affordances of different modes as part of their understanding of rhetoric. Leaving multimodal composition as optional curricular content can give students an incomplete and inaccurate understanding of the discipline.

Third, and perhaps most important, there are larger systemic barriers to multimodal curricular transformation. Tarez Samra Graban et al. (2013) summarize the impediments in the following way: "Campuses are not uniformly equipped, teachers are not technically expert, and curricula dedicated to critical [alphabetic] writing cannot also accommodate multivalent aims as they are delivered through unfamiliar technological contexts" (p. 250). In terms of campus equipment and infrastructure, it is true that some institutions simply do not have the budget or the physical space to create labs/studios that might foster and support multimodal composition. However, there are two counterclaims I would make here. The first is to reemphasize that multimodal compositions do not have to take the form of digital texts—students (and instructors) do not need access to sophisticated computing systems. For example, the kinds of texts that students create in Shipka's class are made from materials that programs can easily provide with available budget or that students can provide as part of their materials cost for any course, like paper, pens, folders, printing, etc. The second is that programs that have made *digital* multimodality a part of their curricula can make use of open-access software or, according to Rory Lee (2018), "expect their students to have their own access to technology. In other words, many majors [in writing] operate according to a Bring-Your-Own-Technology (BYOT) model" (p. 102).[2] Such a policy makes the curriculum flexible, allowing students to bring the materials with which they are the most comfortable to the classroom to engage multimodal composition.

Graban et al.'s concern about teachers' expertise is well taken. While they are specifically addressing the means/materials with which composers make multimodal texts, FYC does have a larger issue when it comes to the expertise of the individuals who deliver our courses. FYC is often taught by those least valued by the institution: graduate teaching assistants, part-time lecturers, or those not on the tenure track. For these individuals who are overworked and underpaid, teaching can be a matter of survival. Additionally, they are more than likely to not have been trained in the discipline of writing studies. FYC programs routinely hire those who are studying or have backgrounds in creative writing, literature, linguistics, and other areas of English studies. Kristine Hansen (2018) writes that this places a lot of pressure on composition program directors, who are "expected to make writing teachers out of dozens of people who have had little to no opportunity to study the discipline of Writing and Rhetoric prior to teaching" (p. 136). It is unrealistic to expect these instructors to embrace multimodal composition enthusiastically when they are perhaps still trying to grasp that the teaching of composition has a history, has theories undergirding its various iterations, and has a growing body of scholarly literature. This is the problem: we know that there are serious impediments to multimodal curricular transformation, not the least of which involve the instructors upon which we routinely rely to deliver FYC to students. We also know that, without multimodal curricular transformation, FYC will become increasingly irrelevant.

What, then, are we to do? How do programs make space for multimodality in composition curricula? What are the methods, processes,

---

2. There are, of course, several problems with this. The digital divide still exists across several demographic lines, and not all students have the same access to the same materials. Too, disability studies scholarship reminds us that not all students access materials in the same way. BYOT may not be the best solution for this programmatic problem, but it is a possible solution, nonetheless.

and strategies by which multimodal curricular transformation can be initiated? The answers to these questions will be productive to those of us who work within composition programs and are interested in making our programs align more closely with contemporary trends in scholarship regarding multimodal composition, but do not know where or how to begin. Systematic inquiry into programs that have successfully entered into multimodal curricular transformation can provide us with possible insights that can be extrapolated to other contexts. To that end, this book will share the results of a mixed-methods research project with the goal of helping readers leave this book not only with a better understanding of multimodality and of curricular revision, but also with

- specific strategies for having the conversations necessary to initiate change,
- models of the documents that support a programmatic ecology in which multimodal composition is vital, and
- understandings of the varied roles that program directors and instructors can play in these processes.

I will argue that multimodal curricular transformation is something that all programs can work toward if we work collaboratively and equitably with instructors to revise the documents that constitute our programs, creating a curricular content that invites multimodality and a programmatic culture that provides the support structures necessary for instructors to accept (if not embrace) multimodal composition.

Chapter 2 asks what the strategies and procedures are by which composition program directors help their programs initiate multimodal curricular transformation. To work toward an answer to that question, I conducted interviews with 10 writing program administrators who have overseen and participated in multimodal curricular transformation at their own institutions.

By reading across interview data, I trace similarities and parallels in the process along the following axes:

1. Motivations and exigences for initiating multimodal curricular transformation,
2. the processes involved in multimodal curricular transformation (including stakeholders involved, documents changed, new initiatives developed, etc.),
3. reasons for resistance to multimodal curricular transformation, and
4. strategies for dealing with resistance to multimodal curricular transformation.

The chapter, thus, presents a set of strategies—collaboration, conversation, decentralization, and professionalization—that can be adopted and adapted within a variety of composition programs. Readers will be able to utilize these in their own contexts and leave with a more nuanced understanding of the processes of multimodal curricular transformation.

Additionally, the interview data revealed that outcomes statements can be a textual site of multimodal curricular transformation through the articulation, renegotiation, and revision of programmatic values, thereby making space for multimodal composition. Taking up this finding, Chapter 3 asks what kinds of curricular content composition programs value currently, and do those values make space for or preclude multimodal composition? I present the analysis of a corpus of outcomes collected from 82 different programs across the field—including those who emphasize multimodal composition and those who do not—yielding a total of 1,353 outcomes. Using a modified version of the outcomes statement released by the Council of Writing Program Administrators (WPA OS) as a coding scheme, I coded each statement to see how frequently certain values, like multimodal composition, appear (or do not). While outcomes statements do not and cannot delineate all of the work done in the composition classroom, they are integral parts of it. They present a definition of and vision for composition to our instructors, our students, and the public, in addition to often providing the means by which we assess our programs. My analysis reveals that, while the frequency with which multimodal composition appears in our published scholarship can suggest otherwise, composition programs remain fairly conservative in content, continuing to emphasize a prescriptive version of alphabetic writing. Thus, the field at large's outcomes present a definition of composition and a set of compositional values that are at odds with our published scholarship. In Chapter 3, I also suggest the ways we might return to, reflect upon, and revise these documents as part of the process of working toward multimodal curricular transformation.

Chapter 4 asks what a transformed multimodal composition curriculum looks like in practice. To answer that question, the chapter utilizes two data points—the interviews referenced in Chapter 2 and programmatic documents from each case study (outcomes statements, sample syllabi, program guides, assignment sheets, etc.)—to detail assignments that instantiate multimodal curricular transformation. The most frequently occurring kind of multimodal assignment in the case study programs was the Remediation Project, in which students shape previously composed material (most often a research project/paper) for a different audience, utilizing a different medium, genre, or constellation of modes. This chapter explores the limitations and affordances of the various iterations of the Remediation Project: Some programs standardize the kinds of remediations that students complete (requiring that all students transform their research papers into digital editorials, for example) while others allow students to make their own choices regarding the materials with which they compose, the audiences for whom they compose, and the vehicles through which their compositions circulate. But while the remediation project can be a beneficial inclusion to the FYC curriculum, adding an assignment is not enough; the case study programs present a consistent vision of composition as multimodal across programmatic documents, including outcomes statements, websites, *and* the assignments delivered to students. The work of multimodal curricular transformation, then, is multitextual.

I end the book by synthesizing my major findings and returning to the overarching question: How can multimodality become an integrated part of composition curricula in the way scholarship argues that it should? My research suggests that changing the content of the FYC curriculum from *writing* to *composition,* using programmatic documents to articulate values that make space for and perhaps require multimodal composition, creating a programmatic culture that allows instructors to deepen their expertise in the field and in multimodality while also allowing them to shape the content of the program are all vital parts of the process of multimodal curricular transformation. Readers will leave this book with strategies for initiating the process in their own contexts, textual models of programmatic documents that support the transformation, and an understanding of the roles that administrators can play in these processes. In other words, multimodal curricular transformation is achievable, and in working toward it, we align ourselves more closely with the discipline, we increase students' rhetorical possibilities, and we position FYC well to serve a vital role in helping students cross contexts and cultures as twenty-first-century meaning-makers.

2
THE PROCESSES OF MULTIMODAL CURRICULAR TRANSFORMATION

As I mentioned in the first chapter of this book, we do not need more individual instructors taking up multimodal composition in their individual classrooms; we need programs to engage in multimodal curricular transformation. Those of us in writing studies and writing program administration are well positioned for this work because the history of FYC can be traced along moments of transformation. Two of these, according to Neal Lerner (2005), occurred in the years 1879–1880 and 1969–1970, in which universities experienced massive influxes of students (p. 188). Within these moments, student populations expanded and diversified, and according to Susan McLeod (2007), "new curricula developed in response" (p. 63). Robert Connors (1997) elaborates: "From the province of a small group of elite students, college education became, during this time, much more available to the masses. The colleges suddenly found themselves with students who needed to be taught to write, who needed to be taught correctness in writing, who needed to know forms, and who could be run through the system in great numbers" (p. 9). In these moments, the composition program was not revised incrementally; it was *transformed* in response to the rhetorical needs—perceived deficits might be a more accurate description—of the expanding student population, redefining the work of composition in the process. McLeod is careful to note that the foundation on which composition programs are built is one tied to formalism and to alphabetic writing. She writes, "first year composition was born under the shadow of remediation and a focus on correctness, a heritage that can create difficulties for present day writing program administrators" (p. 29). These continue to influence our composition programs. To keep us relevant, to keep us *vital,* our programs must be able to revise and transform. Multimodal curricular transformation, a reflective and recursive process of integrating multimodal composition within FYC, will require that we redefine and renegotiate our curricular and programmatic values. This history reminds us that we have done so in the past and that we can do so again.

https://doi.org/10.7330/9781646422135.c002

Programmatic change, however, is difficult. Writing programs "emerge through complex networks of interrelations, depend upon adaptation, fluidity, and the constant motion of discursive systems, are generative and constitutive of diverse rhetorics and discourses, and exhibit a range of other ecological features" (Reiff et al., 2015, p. 4). Change to one part of the programmatic-curricular ecology affects and is affected by the other constituent parts. Scholars in writing program administration have endeavored to theorize curricular revision, situating processes of curricular change along a continuum from local, textual changes, such as the revision of teachers' guides (Graban & Ryan, 2005) to the crafting of a curriculum that exists in a constant state of revision (Brady, 2006; Reid, 2003) to paradigmatic shifts that transform the culture of the program (Hedges, 1996; Hein & Riegel, 2011) to changing perceptions about writing and writing programs outside of the academy (Adler-Kassner, 2008). In practice, this can take various forms. Donna Strickland (2011), for example, advocates for operative management, a kind of reflection that calls us to "notice and investigate our emotional stances toward our work, our beliefs about what constitutes a successful program" (pp. 120–121). E. Shelley Reid (2003) proposes a similar practice, arguing that programs should perceive changing as "an expectation rather than an imposition" (p. 11). In so doing, she argues, we can focus on the process, on existing in a state of changing, which allows the program to "generate a culture of reflective, adaptive practice" (p. 23). These approaches are instantiations of curricular transformation because they recognize that simply achieving change is not the goal. Rather, the goal is an ongoing commitment to making and remaking programs in response to local context, student needs, and disciplinary trends.

To that end, this chapter asks what the strategies and procedures are by which composition programs work toward and initiate multimodal curricular transformation. What does multimodal curricular transformation involve? What does it look like? To answer these questions, I examine 10 case study programs that have enacted multimodal curricular transformation. Thus far, there have been a limited number of investigations into multimodal composition curricula *across* programs. By reading across multiple case studies rather than focusing on individual programs, I locate a compelling set of considerations, developed from multiple contexts, flexible enough to be taken up and adapted in various situations. To choose case studies, I sent a call to the WPA-Listserv, inquiring about programs that had recently revised their FYC programs to make multimodal composition a substantial part of their curricula. Ten individuals responded to that call, and I conducted hour-long interviews with each respondent. The interviews were more formal than informal in that they were "scheduled in advance and [included] some guiding questions" (Dyson & Genishi, 2005, p. 75). I utilized the same guiding questions for each interview, divided into three sections: demographics (teaching faculty, student population, curriculum overview); processes of revision (stakeholders, locations, documents, and any moments of resistance); and definitions and manifestations of multimodality (common assignments). They were, however, loosely structured, which permitted me to ask follow-up questions and follow lines of thought "to put behavior in context" (Seidman, 2006, p. 10) in terms of their motivations for pursuing multimodal curricular transformation; strategies for engaging the process of transformation; and causes for and ways of navigating resistance to multimodal curricular transformation.

To trace similarities and differences in the case studies, I begin this chapter with an overview of programmatic information (including institutional information, teaching faculty demographics, course content, etc.). The variances in case study demography juxtaposed with the consistency of the interview data suggests common features of multimodal curricular transformation that might be extrapolated to other contexts. Then, I detail the various motivations for moving toward multimodal curricular transformation, the most powerful and persuasive of which is making the full available means of persuasion available to students. Some of the case studies I present also utilized a secondary exigence, seizing a kairotic moment of opportunity, revealing that it could be beneficial for individuals who wish to work toward multimodal curricular transformation to be ready for the moment when transformation is most possible. Following that, I outline the processes of multimodal curricular transformation, which, according to these case studies, involves a collaborative revision and remaking of programmatic documents to include and/or make space for multimodal composition. (The importance of these kinds of documents, specifically outcomes statements, will be explored in greater detail in Chapter 3.) Finally, these case studies present a most interesting finding: Resistance to multimodal curricular transformation is not necessarily prohibitive of change. On the contrary, resistance is a vital part of the process, creating the space in which administrators and instructors can have conversations about values (both programmatic and individual). Therefore, readers will leave this chapter with specific strategies that they might invoke should they wish to work toward multimodal curricular transformation in their own programs.

Table 2.1. Case study information

Program Name	Institutional Type	Student Population	Curricular Description after MCT
Program 1	Public college	~18,000	Theme-based focus on academic literacies in first course and public, digital literacies in second course
Program 2	Public college	~16,000	Theme-based, focusing on the role of inquiry in writing
Program 3	Public, land grant, research university	~24,000	Introduction to rhetoric and writing, emphasis on argumentation
Program 4	Public, regional research (R2) university	~20,000	Introduction to rhetoric and writing
Program 5	Public research (R2) university	~24,000	Introduction to rhetoric and writing
Program 6	Private Jesuit university	~8,500	Theme-based, focusing on academic literacies and inquiry
Program 7	Private, Ivy League, research (R1) university	~22,000	Theme-based, writing-in-the-disciplines approach
Program 8	Public research (R1) university (Hispanic-serving institution)	~25,000	Introduction to rhetoric and writing
Program 9	Public liberal arts university	~11,000	Theme-based approach, emphasis on rhetoric
Program 10	Public research (R1) university	~30,000	Introduction to rhetoric and writing

INTRODUCING THE CASE STUDY PROGRAMS

Information regarding institutional size, teaching faculty, and overall programmatic foci suggests that multimodal curricular transformation can be initiated *in various institutional settings and within various curricular structures* because the 10 case studies differ in size, instructor/student population, and focus. See Tables 2.1 and 2.2 for a brief summary.

There are a few conclusions we might draw from this information regarding institutional and program type (Table 2.1) and the make-up of the instructional staff (Table 2.2). First, multimodal curricular transformation does not only take place at R1 institutions staffed primarily by graduate students in writing studies; it takes place in various programs with instructors of various rank and background. Second, multimodal curricular transformation does not require a specific curricular focus—these programs house courses that exist along a continuum from theme-based approaches to introductions to writing studies. The variances here are juxtaposed with the similarities in the interview data; the motivations, exigences, processes, and strategies for transformation in these different contexts were strikingly similar. These similarities can be extrapolated from these case studies, helping readers work toward multimodal curricular transformation in their own contexts.

Motivations and Exigences for Multimodal Curricular Transformation

In all interviews, I asked participants why they chose to initiate multimodal curricular transformation in their programs. According to the directors, there was a range of motivations, which included:

- **Acknowledging and honoring the current literacy practices of and future literacy expectations for students within the program**. Per the director of Program 8, "We really wanted to focus in on digital literacy, because we felt like that's the environment that our students are in, and that they will continue to be living in and working in. They're going to have to, at some point, engage with multiliteracies." Similarly, at Program 7, the director mentioned that graduating students wished "they had had some more experience in public writing. Not having that experience in public writing, they felt, was a kind of deficit. This [the curricular transformation] was also a way to really give them experience in public writing on the web."
- **Being aware of and noticing trends in writing studies scholarship**. The director of Program 6 stated that "part of it also had to do with the fact that, from those of us who were going to Cs and other things, we were seeing that the field is changing. It's not just the five-paragraph essay, which since I began teaching in the seventies, people were talking about people needing to move away from."

However, the most frequent and *salient* motivation was a *desire to align the goals and focus of the program with an understanding of FYC-as-rhetoric.* In defining the content of FYC as the study and practice of rhetoric, programs invite students to "do what rhetoricians have been suggesting for over a thousand years," which involves utilizing "all available means of persuasion" (Selfe & Selfe, 2008, p. 84). For example, in talking through the revisions made to the program in which he works, the director at Program 2 mentioned that "audience awareness is really at the heart of a composition program . . . figuring out how to respond in a rhetorical situation is more important than any specific writing assignment." Program 6's director furthered this, stating quite succinctly, "If you're going to be in the field of teaching composition and rhetoric, rhetoric is not only a written construct. It belongs to the visual medium. It belongs to the oral medium. It belongs to non-alphabetic text." These directors made it quite clear: rhetoric is (a part of) the content of composition, rhetoric involves more than just words on a page, and therefore it is necessary to

Table 2.2. Teaching faculty information

Program Name	Teaching Faculty Rank	Area(s) of Expertise
Program 1	Mostly staffed by adjuncts (70%); a few tenure-track (TT) faculty and graduate students (MA level)	Literature, creative writing, writing studies
Program 2	Most sections staffed by adjuncts; remainder staffed by graduate students (MA level)	Most adjuncts are MFAs; graduate students can be studying literature, literacy, or writing studies
Program 3	Primarily staffed by graduate students (MA and PhD level)	Literature, creative writing, writing studies
Program 4	Balanced among full-time lecturers, part-time lecturers, graduate students, and tenure-track faculty	Literature, linguistics, writing studies, creative writing, English education
Program 5	Primarily staffed by graduate students (MA and PhD level)	Literature, creative writing, writing studies
Program 6	95% of sections are staffed by full-time and part-time lecturers	Literature, creative writing, writing studies
Program 7	Tenure-track faculty	Across all disciplines in the university
Program 8	Primarily staffed by graduate students	Literature, creative writing, writing studies
Program 9	Tenure-track faculty	English studies
Program 10	Primarily staffed by graduate students (MA and PhD level)	Literature, creative writing, writing studies

endeavor toward multimodal curricular transformation. In the words of Program 10's director:

> It goes back to the available means of persuasion, doesn't it? At the point where we had a pen and paper, that was the available means of persuasion, but it is no longer that. We have available at our fingertips, right here in front of me [referencing her computer] or even on my phone, means of persuasion that are multiple. If we don't encourage using those and teach people how to use those to persuade, then we're not doing rhetoric. We're not composing. It's a matter of the available means of persuasion. I'm a huge fan of Richard Lanham. He defines rhetoric as the economics of human attention structures. I think that's a beautiful definition of rhetoric. It's an economic situation, and it has to do with cost and availability of things and getting attention. Human attention structures are our five senses. Those are the ways that you get attention.

This is a motivation to transform content of the composition curriculum in such a way that it will make critical interventions in the persuasive potentialities of students who move through the program. Within this kind of multimodal-rhetorical curriculum, a curriculum for which contemporary scholarship strongly advocates, students cultivate "a better sense of how to adapt, how to communicate, how to research, how to deliver messages to various audiences, how to meet different rhetorical situations. I would like to think that it gave them a wider array of options for how to communicate," according to the director of Program 8.

In expanding these possibilities, these programs help students better prepare for the communicative landscape in which they will live and work. As I have written previously, "By changing the literacy work of the composition program, by changing the kinds of texts that students create, by changing the audiences for whom they create those texts, we position ourselves well to make our students not only better composers, but more active and engaged citizens in the world" (Bearden, 2019b, p. 79). Those who are interested in including multimodal composition in their programs ought to take this finding into consideration. Multimodal curricular transformation, for these case studies, was not (only) an effort to include digital literacy or flashy technologies; multimodal curricular transformation operates from and initiates as a response to an understanding of composition-as-rhetoric. Per these directors, the role of the composition program is to help students cultivate fluency in means of persuasion/communication that are multiple.

Some participants also reported that a simultaneous exigence made multimodal curricular transformation possible, demonstrating a strategy that can be taken up by other WPAs who wish to see their programs through a similar transformation. Co-exigences varied, but the strategic decision to seize those kairotic moments was consistent. For example, the directors at Programs 1 and 2 mentioned that the primary exigence that would eventually lead to multimodal curricular transformation was a desire for stronger programmatic coherence and consistency. At Program 2, the director knew that overall revisions were necessary, because in reviewing "all of the syllabi, hardly any of [the instructors] were including course learning outcomes of any kind. Only 30% included outcomes. So, I wanted to get something in place—and get it in place quickly—so that people started thinking about it [the composition course] as part of a larger program, rather than an individual course."

Using programmatic documents, like outcomes and syllabi, to cohere the program also allowed the director of Program 2 to "put an assessment in place, [because] everybody had to be shooting for the same thing in order for it to be valid." As part of that process, the director implemented a digital portfolio, not just because of the ease of collection for assessment purposes, but because creating a *digital* portfolio "enlivens the rhetorical canon" for students. Thus, while the primary exigence for Program 2 was coherence, the director was able to use that moment to implement the digital portfolio and the rhetorical practices entailed therein, thereby initiating multimodal curricular transformation.

The curricular revisions that would eventually lead to multimodal curricular transformation were inspired by a desire for program coherence at Program 1 as well. The director there stated that she "wanted to try to make more of a distinction between the two courses" required by the program because distinguishing the two courses would allow the program to shift the focus of the second course to public, digital literacies. According to the director, this was beneficial for students because it aligned the program with what Bill Cope and Mary Kalantzis (2000) term students' *situated practices*, the "meaningful [literacy] practices within a community . . . based on their backgrounds and experiences" (p. 33). Program 1's director phrased it in the following way: "Cutting through all the bullshit, digital literacies are where students live. We have to go in these directions even if we're flailing around and failing miserably. We have to be able to ask these really hard questions. What does it mean to live in a world when we're constantly looking at screens and we're all composing with digital media to various degrees? And what role does first-year writing, this ubiquitous course that very few people want to take or teach, have in these new literacies?" Focusing on public, digital literacies in the second course of the FYC sequence, then, became a way for this program to validate and embrace the multimodal literacy practices that students bring with them to the classroom, a move made possible through the larger curricular revision goal of programmatic coherence.

These manifested differently in other programs but reflected the larger overall trend of strategically seizing coexigences. For example, the director at Program 4 utilized the publication of the most recent revisions to the WPA outcomes statement released in 2014 (which I explore in greater detail in the next section of this chapter) as both *exigence and ethos* for programmatic revisions that would lead to multimodal curricular transformation. In our interview, he stated, "We were revising the outcomes anyway, and we decided that, if we're going to have fluid, dynamic, up-to-the-moment fresh outcomes, living outcomes, how the hell are we gonna do that if we're not honoring the times, if we're not recognizing the moment that we live in? You know? Like, let's not forget that we're in the now, right? So that's what I feel like multimodality does. It says, 'We're noticing the world we live in or noticing the world our students live in.'" In this scenario, the program seized the kairotic moment that occurred at the intersection of the program's commitment to revising its outcomes and the release of the WPA OS 3.0. The program was therefore able to include multimodal composing as a part of the program's content.

Three other program directors (Programs 5, 8, & 9) stated that the coexigence for curricular revisions that would eventually lead to multimodal curricular transformation was a form of institutional financial support. At Program 5, this took the form of resources that made it possible to "hire grad students to be digital writing consultants and to support teachers integrating digital technologies, for us to get certain kinds of technological tools, etc. That was definitely really helpful in the time period that we were really trying to make that shift. A lot of this was folded into the training for new teachers, but we also did some day-long or day-and-a-half-long workshops for more experienced instructors about the new curriculum and the new resources. We were able to offer ongoing support after that as to how they could implement these things." To reiterate, curricular revisions were initiated and supported by institutional funding. However, the director here made use of that moment to create programmatic infrastructures (professional development workshops and training, hiring graduate assistants, etc.) that would help make multimodal curricular transformation both possible and sustainable. These infrastructures help to shift the culture of the program: in this program multimodal composition became embedded in the program's documents (mission statement, outcomes, etc.), a vital part of teacher training and development, and supported by the existence of a digital studio. Similarly, Programs 8 and 9 made use of statewide grants to support curricular revisions. At Program 9, the director stated:

> I got a ton of money to revise the program . . . to the tune of about $350,000 a year. Tons of money. That lasted for four years. Those were the good years. And then what I did was I rolled out the program over three years, so I did a third, and I took my best instructors and people who I knew could kind of roll with the punches and all of that. And we changed over their curriculum and got them trained and up and running, and then the next year we did that plus another third. And then the final year was the final third.

It is no surprise that funding increases the possibilities for and sustainability of curricular initiatives, especially when those curricular initiatives involve multiple media (see Porter, 2009; Selfe, 2005). However, while a surplus of financial resources was the exigence that made curricular revisions possible, it was the strategic choices and movements of a director who believed that the program needed to be brought into the twenty-first century that led to multimodal curricular transformation. I want to be clear: Supplementary financial resources are *not* necessary to the process(es) of multimodal curricular transformation—several of these programs initiated significant programmatic change without such support. The more important takeaway here for those who are interested in working toward this in their own contexts is that, for these programs, the funds provided an exigence, a serendipitous kairotic moment for the directors leading these programs to seize strategically, seeking out various moments of opportunity that they can leverage toward transformation. This preparedness, combined with the motivation to craft a more rhetorically capacious program, these case studies reveal, can be a vital part of the revision processes that lead multimodal curricular transformation, which I will explore in greater detail in the following section.

Process(es) of Curricular Transformation

In interviews, I asked participants about the processes of multimodal curricular transformation: what it looked like in practice, who was involved, how they were involved, how the revisions manifested, etc. Two features emerged from reading across the interview data:

1. **The process must be collaborative**. The case studies suggest that this feminist administrative strategy provides stakeholders with the opportunity to shape the program in which they work, bringing them into the reflective programmatic remaking that is part of multimodal curricular transformation.

2. **Curricular revisions take place within documents**. Participants made sure to mention that the revision of template syllabi, outcomes statements, assignment sheets, and other kinds of programmatic documents allowed them to carve out space for multimodal composition within their curricula.

In what follows, I will present these insights in further detail, insights that composition program directors and other individuals who work within FYC can consider within their own contexts as they work toward multimodal curricular transformation.

Collaboration Is Key

The case studies prove that this kind of curricular transformation is collaborative and involves many stakeholders within composition programs. This helps to increase transparency, distribute authority, and provide the instructors within the program the opportunity to shape the curricula they deliver to students. All 10 of the directors to whom I spoke acknowledged that the curricular revisions that led to transformation were not the effort of a single individual. The director at Program 10 stated simply that any curricular revision to their program "is always collaborative. Changes like this are never top down." These processes enact feminist administrative principles, which, according to Goodburn and Leverenz (1998), include "nonhierarchical collaboration, shared leadership, and the recognition of multiple sources of authority" (p. 277). Feminist approaches to administration resist and operate against patriarchal administrative models in which revision can be seen changing individuals through a demonstration of power, instead emphasizing "community, shared responsibility, and open exchange of information, ideas, and criticism" (Gunner, 2002, p. 254). Programs that utilize these approaches resist Ed White's (1991) mantra of "use it [power] or lose it," validating the many and varied voices present in the program. For the programs that are the focus of this chapter, collaboration took place in various venues.

Sometimes collaboration took place in program-wide meetings, which allowed for the teaching faculty working in the program to participate in the process(es) of curricular revision and program-(re)making. For example, the director of Program 7 said, "We think of ourselves as a giant lab. . . . Everyone has PhDs in different disciplines, but we do a shared curriculum. We get together. We talk about curriculum. We look at the results. We assess the results and so forth and then we make a decision." That decision-making process involves "lots of meetings" in which the "40 full-time faculty get together and discuss and argue and so forth." With diverse teaching faculty comes diverse needs and opinions, and these meetings provided a low-stakes, informal venue for those voices to be heard. Similarly, Program 10 made space for informal collaboration during monthly professional development meetings. During one of those sessions, the director stated that the teaching faculty

> discussed the current portfolio requirements, and then we took those to the composition committee, which has about seven or eight members. The composition committee took all the input from professional development conversation and boiled it down. Then, they took it back to the general teaching population and said, "What do you think?" They messed with it, said what they liked, said what they didn't like. We did some things. We took it back to the comp committee, and then the comp committee tweaked all of the suggestions. Then we put it out as a general document, and I think that all of that process happened in a spring semester. Then in the following fall semester, everybody was using those new digital portfolio requirements.

The iterative nature of the revision process provided many opportunities for the teaching faculty to participate in determining the shape of the transformed multimodal composition curriculum rather than imposing that curriculum onto the teaching faculty.

Program 2 also involved the program's composition committee to seek feedback as a part of a collaborative process of working toward multimodal curricular transformation *with* teaching faculty. Part of the program's curricular revision involved developing new outcomes, which "went through a process in the composition committee. They were reviewed; there was some discussion; there were some focus groups." The director initiated this process, mentioning in his interview, "I put together a list from the CWPA website [the WPA OS]. I brought in some suggestions. I distributed them on a GoogleDoc and asked people to weigh in. Then we met and discussed those in the committee itself. It started in November and concluded in May. They were pushed out the following year." In this way, while it was the director's vision to proceed with new outcomes, the shape of the final outcomes was a *collaborative* product. Several other programs utilized their composition committees as a way to allow the teaching faculty responsible for delivering curricula the opportunity to shape those curricula. At Program 6, "the English department members who teach composition were all invited to a meeting to discuss what the learning outcomes were regardless of rank. The meetings, which I chaired, had people who were hired to teach writing from the non-tenure-stream lines and the tenure-stream lines." In those meetings, the director of Program 6 projected a Google Doc of the draft outcomes to make sure that she was capturing the responses accurately. After those meetings, the outcomes were "circulated to the department for comment before it was forwarded to the head of all the core curriculum." These programs reveal that collaboration can take many forms (in large meetings, in small committees, etc.) and that there is not one correct way to collaborate with teaching faculty.

Program 4 collaborated with its instructors using a survey, which simultaneously encouraged the teaching faculty to voice their concerns about the previous iteration of the program and allowed them to shape the future of the program. The director described the process thusly: "We sent the survey out to all 50 of our instructional staff asking about the two courses and also about the efficacy of the outcomes for articulating what's important to us in these courses. So, we circulated the program-wide survey. We got 33 people to complete it, I think. Pretty high. We felt pretty satisfied with that. It confirmed for us this sense that the existing outcomes weren't doing the clarifying work that they needed to do." To reiterate, the specific venue of collaboration is less important than what collaboration as a programmatic practice invites: increased transparency, distributed authority in a decentered program, and the opportunity for teaching faculty to shape the program in which they work. The director of Program 10 made it quite clear that this was the most important part of the process. I asked her what advice she would offer to individuals who might be working toward multimodal curricular transformation in their own contexts. Her response to that question was to "involve everybody. Be collaborative. Any changes that are possible for you to make, make them collaboratively. Get all kinds of input from the stakeholders. It's just like good assessment. Good assessment involves all the stakeholders. Involve the teachers who are actually on the ground with 25 students in their classes." For those who wish to implement any curricular revisions, and especially multimodal curricular transformation, collaborating with teaching faculty is a necessary part of the process.

Curricular Reimaginings Take Place within Documents

Work at the intersection of rhetorical genre studies and writing program administration reveals the power that documents have in shaping programmatic practices, possibilities, and identities (see Bawarshi & Reiff, 2010). According to Tarez Samra Graban and Kathleen J. Ryan (2005), "the (re)production of curricular documents provides a space for initiating and sustaining discussions on high-stakes topics . . . and it also promotes reform by reconstructing the programs they represent" (pp. 89–90). In other words, the revision of programmatic documents can lead to a kind of reflective practice in which programs can make space for new kinds of curricular content. This proved to be true for these case studies, because one of the most frequently addressed programmatic documents in these interviews was the outcomes statement: *The process of multimodal curricular transformation began in most of these programs by reviewing the program's outcomes.* For example, the director of Program 5 reported that at the beginning of the revision process, "we reviewed our outcomes. I remember we did some paring down. At that point, our program had 20 outcomes. Too many to assess. I think the primary one that we worked on was the digital and multimodal rhetoric outcome." These textual revisions allowed this program to return to and reevaluate its values, and in that textual-reflective space, the program was able to center multimodality within its composition curriculum.

In reflecting upon the outcomes statement as a document and its role in curriculum-making, several programs made use of the outcomes statement adopted by the Council of Writing Program Administrators

(WPA OS) as a source of invention and/or acknowledged the role that the national document played/plays in shaping their local curricula. This document "attempts to both represent and regularize writing programs' priorities for first-year composition . . . articulat[ing] what composition teachers nationwide have learned from practice, research, and theory" (Council of Writing Program Administrators, 2014). Efforts to craft a document like the WPA OS emerged from a conversation that began on the WPA-L. Ed White (2005) had found at his own institution that "each teacher was more or less on his or her own, at best guided by a few generalizations about the kind of reading material and writing assignments to use in each course," and that, while there were "principles and practices for the hiring of composition instructors, there were no such principles for what those instructors might actually teach" (p. 4). His question about creating some kind of consensus document regarding what we would like students to know and do by the end of FYC functioned as a call for "a document that circulates and codifies the basic tenets that undergird our discipline's pedagogical goals and assumptions about FYC" (Olson, 2013, p. 29). This document would attempt to answer the question of what goes on/should go on in FYC. A multivocal conversation and collaborative composing process ensued. The Outcomes Collective, those in charge of drafting and seeking feedback on the document, viewed "each conference and meeting [as] an opportunity to bring in new voices" because they "wanted this to be a document adopted and adapted by as many people as possible" (Rhodes et al., 2005, p. 10). The goal of the WPA OS was not to impose national standards on local programs, but to examine "what we have in common, what best ideas and best practices we could all agree on" (p. 11). The resulting document reflects consensus through disciplinary knowledge, naming and synthesizing what the field of composition studies knows about writing and the teaching of writing "from practice, research, and theory" (Council of Writing Program Administrators). In this way, the WPA OS "legitimizes and justifies writing pedagogies and the work of the local WPA; it facilitates conversations about writing instruction and values; and it guides curriculum design, teacher development, and assessment practices" (Dryer et al., 2014, p. 131). As such, it is at once an articulation of values, a dialogue, and an *invitation* for local curricular revision. Kathleen Blake Yancey (2012), for example, writes that "individual campuses could take them up and revise them toward local outcomes, thus providing for both local mission and intent and at the same time for articulation with a larger context" (p. 173). Its flexibility and adaptability are part of the document's strengths. In other words, it defines a version of composition informed by disciplinary knowledge and outlines programmatic practices by which that version of composition is enacted.

To that end, many scholars have written about the role of the WPA OS in curricular revisions: as a source of ethos (Grettano et al., 2013; Harrison, 2013; Jacobsen et al., 2013; Pettipiece & Everett, 2013), as a source of inventional material (Dunn et al., 2013; Gresham, 2013; Hokanson, 2005; McClure, 2005; Wilhoit, 2005), and in emphasizing the importance of rhetoric within the composition curriculum (Maid & D'Angelo, 2013). The director of Program 9 utilized the WPA OS to leverage the inclusion of rhetoric as a way to make space for multimodal composition, stating, "As I think a lot of people do, we started with the WPA outcomes and then kind of modified them from there. I feel really passionate about having a rhetoric-based curriculum. That's probably where I had the biggest personal-professional imprint on the program." The WPA OS provided inventional material derived from a professional organization, one that emphasizes rhetoric, that the program could then personalize for its local context. Now that the WPA OS (version 3.0) threads multimodal composition throughout the document, WPAs and programs who are interested in multimodal curricular transformation in their programs might look to that document as a starting point for revising their own outcomes and programs. Program 10 made use of this new definition. The director there stated, "the new WPA outcomes—now [at the time of the interview] they're two or three years old—have large paragraphs of explanation of each of the individual outcomes. We edited that down and wanted it to be a sentence or two that teachers would understand, that students could understand maybe with some more conversation. We wanted to make sure that they were intelligible and brief."

In addition to being inventional material, the WPA OS also served as a source of ethos in the process of curricular transformation for a few of the case study programs. The director of Program 8 invoked the WPA OS, stating, "That's how we showed them [administrators and reluctant teaching faculty] that we belong to this bigger world beyond our campus. It wasn't necessarily that we used the WPA Outcomes to change our curriculum, but we brought the WPA Outcomes along with it and kept checking ourselves in that regard." Like this director, those who are involved in the process of multimodal curricular transformation can make the argument that programmatic revisions are not idiosyncratic but rather are positioned within a national network of ideas and best practices, imbuing those revisions with disciplinary authority.

Similarly, the director at Program 3 chose to adopt the WPA OS because "I needed a stronger, more professional, associational set of outcomes." In invoking the WPA OS to situate and contextualize changes to the local outcomes, both of these programs drew on the rhetorical possibilities of documents to create change. This is a particularly savvy move for those involved in multimodal curricular transformation because, as I have mentioned, the most recent iteration of the document defines the content of first-year composition in a way that centers multimodal composition (see Dryer et al., 2014).

This information provides useful takeaways for those interested in performing this work in/for their own programs. First, these case studies reveal that programmatic documents play an integral role in curricular transformation. These directors specifically mentioned the outcomes statement as the site of this work (I explore outcomes and their possible role in transformation in Chapter 3), but it is important to remember that the rhetorical work of a program is spread across many different kinds of texts: program websites, teachers' guides, assignment sheets, and grading rubrics. All of these are places where we might make space for (or preclude) multimodal composition, and all of these are places where we can make clear arguments about the role of multimodality in FYC. Second, when revising these documents, WPAs could strategically draw upon national documents as sources of ethos and inventional material: Several directors referenced using the WPA OS to contextualize their revisions and explain why the revisions were helping to align the program with disciplinary best practices. Other kinds of documents and statements could be invoked as well, such as the NCTE position statements on twenty-first-century literacies and multimodal literacies. These textual-rhetorical strategies could make multimodal curricular transformation possible and sustainable in certain contexts. However, those who initiate this work should anticipate a certain amount of resistance, which I will explore in greater detail in the next section.

RESISTANCE TO MULTIMODAL CURRICULAR TRANSFORMATION

Changes to curricula can be met with resistance from those who teach within the program. We know from research that instructors resist new or different curricula most frequently when the new content counters or threatens their personal construct and self-efficacy (Dryer, 2012; Ebest, 2005). And some instructors, according to Jennifer Grouling (2015), resist the *theory* informing curricula because they "are looking for practical advice to the problems of the classroom, which they see as separate from theory." Teaching is already a difficult process; adding elements that are radically different or that seem impractical can cause instructors to balk. Multimodality seems to be particularly troublesome in this regard. Some instructors believe that multimodal composition could "get in the way of learning good [alphabetic] writing and argument skills" (Hill & Ericsson, 2014, p. 147). To these individuals, alphabetic writing is more rigorous. As I mentioned in Chapter 1, others might conflate "multimodal" with "digital," and so resistance to this curriculum and pedagogical approach could be rooted in typical sources of resistance to technology. Moerschell (2009) argues that, for some instructors, technology is a source of anxiety *outside* of the classroom and would be even more so *within* it. With this scholarship in mind, I suspected that the directors that I interviewed for this project would have dealt with resistance to multimodal curricular transformation, and I was correct. To briefly forecast, the sources of resistance that these directors mentioned included concerns about teacherly ethos/expertise/authority within a multimodal composition curriculum *and* questions about how multimodality fits within the content of composition. Understanding these sources allowed WPAs to engage feminist pragmatic rhetorical strategies to operate within resistance and see resistance as a productive part of curricular transformation.

In certain programs, instructors resisted multimodal curricular transformation because multimodal composition appeared to threaten their teacherly expertise, ethos, or identity. For example, the director at Program 5 stated that resistance to the changes there stemmed from teaching faculty having been "trained in one model and had been teaching one way for a long time." To these individuals, multimodal composition fell outside of that model. I find this is one of the most logical tensions in the process(es) of multimodal curricular transformation, which requires additional effort from instructors who do not perceive themselves to be trained in teaching and assessing multimodal projects. At Program 2, the director stated, "People claim accurately that this is additional labor for which they are not being paid. They don't want to learn a new platform. They didn't get sufficient training for it. And I can't really argue with that, because it's all true."

This is especially the case for adjunct faculty who comprise most of the instructional staff at Program 1. The director there said, "Until you've done it, it's just scary as hell. You don't know. Your students are going to know more than you? What about that? Is that okay? And if you're already contingent faculty, it's even less okay." In these programs, instructors felt that they lacked the ethos (or perhaps the self-efficacy, per Sally Barr Ebest, 2005) to participate within a transformed multimodal composition curriculum. Even when the instructors resisted technology as a part of the overall curricular transformation, those concerns arose from larger concerns about teacherly authority. Program 5's director summarized it thusly: "A lot of it [resistance] was just a fear of lack of knowledge." Instructors in Program 5 were stating, "I don't know the technology. I don't know how to evaluate or grade this kind of thing. That isn't what my training is for as an English teacher." Multimodal curricular transformation, to these instructors, seemed to require a different kind of expertise.

This is especially the case when it comes to assessment practices. At Program 10, multimodality was perceived as so radically different from the traditional content of composition that the teaching faculty could not conceptualize what it would look like in the curriculum or how to assess it. The director there stated, "The teachers were saying 'The requirements don't work. How do we fit the requirement of 22 pages? How do we count a multimodal project as pages?'" Assessment of student work and instructor expertise/ethos are inextricably linked. Instructors can resist curricular transformation if they do not feel immediately prepared to respond to and evaluate multimodal projects. Program 4's director mentioned this kind of resistance in our conversation about names and naming. This program is one of the few that I have encountered in my research that actually includes the word "multimodal/ity" within its program's guiding principles and outcomes. According to the director, this posed a problem because the term "made people the most nervous, like 'Do I know what this is? Do I know if my students are doing it? Do I know how to sponsor that?'" These concerns reinforce what Isaacs (2018), Schiavone (2017), and others have found: While our scholarship discusses and theorizes multimodality often and at length, that same scholarship can have little impact on the day-to-day work of individual teachers who may not have the time or the resources to stay abreast of disciplinary advances. If they cannot, it is difficult for them to perceive themselves as possessing the expertise/ethos necessary for multimodal curricular transformation.

Not least, some instructors resist multimodal curricular transformation because they believe multimodal composition to be outside the content of FYC, which is yet another challenge to their teacherly ethos or authority. Dylan Dryer (2012) argues that asking instructors to teach concepts that are (still) nebulous to them can lead to "considerable anxiety about—and frequent hostility toward" those concepts (p. 421). This was the case in the programs that are the focus of this chapter as well. For example, in discussing the varying reactions to the inclusion of multiliteracy goals, the director of Program 9 recounted, "A lot of people were like 'I'm already doing this. I got it. I'm on it.' Other people were going 'over my dead body. No way. . . .' Other people were going 'I'll do this, but I just don't know how. I'm just really freaked out by this.' It was a profound paradigm shift in the program and the department for people."

Such a quote illustrates that multimodal curricular transformation can be perceived as threatening or intimidating because it appears to be radically different from their conception of composition. According to Meaghan Brewer (2020), these conceptions are inseparable from one's teacherly identity and pedagogical approach because they "are always ideological in that they are reflections of the worldviews of individuals and groups and always political in that they privilege certain groups or literacy practices while marginalizing and excluding others" (p. 25). If multimodality is both nebulous to instructors *and* at odds with those instructors' conceptions of literacy and composition, then resistance is sure to follow. Program 1's director said simply, "What kind of works against multimodality is that it's not the traditional Research Paper." At Program 7, some instructors lamented the fact that multimodal composition is not an "academic argument." They also argued, "That isn't writing. How is that writing?" The director at Program 3 faced this kind of resistance as well, mentioning that "faculty in other departments were telling my Chair, 'Well, I don't know what y'all are doing in [the required writing course], but students are just making videos." For these individuals, multimodality does not fall within their conception of composition: it is not considered writing, and it does not possess the perceived rigor of academic discourse. Perceiving alphabetic writing as the sole content of FYC is a fundamental misconception of FYC programs, and the discipline of writing studies overall (see Downs & Wardle, 2007). Therefore, while resistance based in the supposed rigor of alphabetic writing is rooted in a misunderstanding of what it means to study and teach composition, it is still resistance to change, to making progress toward multimodal curricular transformation.

In reviewing these interviews, it is evident that while resistance can manifest in various ways, the sources of resistance stemmed from two interrelated categories: (a) misconceptions about the content of FYC, which can and should include multimodal composition, and (b) threats to self-efficacy as an instructor of composition (including ethos, expertise, and authority). The benefit of locating these is that, in understanding the source of resistance to multimodal curricular transformation, we can begin to theorize the process of dealing with it. While Sally Barr Ebest

(2005) reveals that "overcoming resistance is a complex, multi-layered process" (p. 99), the directors that I interviewed for this project success-fully negotiated, navigated, *and utilized* resistance as a vital part of the process of multimodal curricular transformation. Across case studies, these directors utilized collaborative administrative models and what Ryan and Graban (2009) call feminist pragmatic rhetoric, which assumes that "resistance is not antithetical to the learning goals of first-year composition" (p. W278). The authors utilize this standpoint to "embrace resistance as a disciplinary and pedagogical aim" (p. W278), not something that needs to be eradicated. There are three interrelated facets of this approach: "[a] As feminists we are dissatisfied with enacting Foucauldian disciplinary measures because we value knowledge gained experientially and dialogically, and we recognize how subjectivity shapes acts of knowledge making to inform communication. [b] As rhetoricians we find it counterproductive to capitulate because we value our discipline and recognize knowledge making as contextualized, goal-directed communication. [c] And as pragmatists, we think it irresponsible to not react [to resistance] because we want to use our disciplinary knowledge to create good programs" (p. W280). In practice, this means "crediting one another [program directors and instructors] with the belief that we can (re)position and (re)learn, and that we are capable of choosing to do so" (p. W289).

Another way to frame this strategy might be through the lens of Lisa Blankenship's (2019) rhetorical empathy, which combines "rhetoric as a strategic use of symbol systems . . . [and] empathy as both a *conscious, deliberate attempt to understand an Other* and the emotions that can result from such attempts" (p. 7, emphasis added). These directors are not only listening to persuade but also listening to hear what instructors value and to find connections with those values. This feminist pragmatic rhetorical strategy uses resistance as a moment of opportunity. Within this framework, resistance is inevitable, but it is also simultaneously *manageable and productive*, because in embracing resistance, program directors and other stakeholders within programs can have meaningful, reflective conversations about programmatic and individual pedagogical values, student needs, and disciplinary perspectives, wherein those that might resist curricular innovations can find agency and voice.

The directors in these programs embraced resistance as part of multimodal curricular transformation. This was particularly effective in clarifying the role of multimodality in the content of FYC. For example, Program 7's director stated, "Yes: we have resistance, but without resistance we'd have nothing. I really like that we argue about things," because arguing "pretty much ensures that there's nothing we can take for granted." Echoing this sentiment, the director at Program 10 mentioned that disagreements and tensions can "get worked out in the big group conversations." To her, these moments of resistance provide(d) the space to raise "pedagogical questions and also public questions for a writing program" to consider. At Program 3, the director used these moments as an opportunity to initiate conversation. To the claim that "students at [Program 3] can't write," the director responds with, "Well, what do you mean? Do you mean that they can't write like you? What constitutes 'good' writing?" Instead of dismissing these claims as nonproductive, the director refocused the conversation on *values*: "I just ask them to step outside of their question a bit and to look at it. What constitutes 'good' to you? Does it mean perfect? If it means perfect, then you would just want us to be error hunters and take the student's writing and mark it up. I know from 30 years of composition theory in tutoring and teaching that marking grammar does not necessarily result in subsequently better products from students." This strategy of examining the values at the center of the claim invites those with whom the director engages to confront and consider alternative (and more accurate) constructs of composition.

Approaching such conversations with this approach can work to clarify the assumption/misconception that multimodal curricular transformation requires technological expertise. For example, the director at Program 6 stated that she believed teaching faculty will resist multimodality if they perceive it as requiring that they learn electronic or digital media. In those moments, the director reiterated to the instructors in her program, "We don't mean that you have to learn how to do a podcast yourself. We have an IT group on campus who will help with that technical instruction." Similarly, Program 10's director reported, "I think the problem is when people think, 'I have to have students make a full-length feature film.' . . . No. You don't have to be an expert in something digital to make this assignment a little bit multimodal." These directors strategically used the conversations that emerged from resistance to correct that misconception, and in clarifying misconceptions, the director at Program 9 attempted to persuade the instructors with whom she worked to "just try one thing." In describing this approach, she mentioned wanting the instructors in her program to

> work with something that you know and that you're comfortable with. That really helped me. I was thinking about all of this as, "oh my god—everyone has to do these super complex multimedia projects, and I can't do them. How am I going to teach teachers to do them?" So that's how I got to "just try one thing." You don't even have to do it all semester. Just do one thing.

> That's what I tell people that are resistant, hostile, overwhelmed. Just try
> one thing. Then, we can build up from there. You know, here's a menu of
> options, and here's a whole variety of kinds of support for you to do that,
> because we do very intensive professional development. And my job is to
> develop those ideas and the support and the materials and the resources.

Over time these efforts changed the culture of the program to one that
embraced multimodal composition. The director at Program 5 utilized
this as well. He stated, "One of the first ways I dealt with resistance was
to make it clear that you don't have to make huge changes all at once.
I encouraged people with 'Let's try out one thing. Perhaps you've been
doing everything on paper. I'm going to show you another way to try
out peer response. Just do that.'" Taking the time to clarify misconceptions regarding multimodal curricula is particularly effective in the long
term because multimodal composition does not require individual instructors to become experts in specific technologies. Indeed, it would
be unwise to require specific ones because technologies quickly become
obsolete (see Fitzpatrick, 2011 or Sheridan et al., 2012). The director
of Program 5 went on to elaborate: "One of the biggest arguments I
make [in favor of multimodality] is first that we're teaching a course that
purports to prepare people for a lifetime of communicating effectively.
Increasingly, we're not really sure what communication is going to look
like in the future, but we're pretty sure it's not going to be black letters
on a printed, white page. If we're going to get student buy-in to this
course as meaningful for a lifetime of composing and actually follow up
on that goal, then we need to give them some experience with thinking
critically about those texts."

Thus, it appears that part of multimodal curricular transformation
involves defining (or perhaps clarifying) the role of multimodality within
FYC to help instructors find their way into the changes. If, as the director
of Program 5 suggests, the goal of FYC is to teach a way of theorizing
the practice of communicating effectively, then multimodality allows us
to embrace a fuller means of communication. In this way, conversations
that navigate misconceptions about writing become a strategic move in
dealing with resistance to transformation. The director at Program 2 has
a practiced argument for conversations in which misconceptions about
writing can be righted: he makes the point "that virtually all meaningful
communication in 2017 [the time of the interview] happens online, and
that composition courses should be to some extent about communication, and to avoid the primary means of communication in that class
is irresponsible." Such an argument clearly outlines the relationship
between multimodality and the full available means of communication,

revealing and reinforcing that part of multimodal curricular transformation involves centering rhetoric within the composition curriculum, allowing students to use the communicative resources that are available and apt. Too, this particular director emphasized that such transformation is necessary, because "the digital native is a myth. Young people aren't magically born knowing how to manipulate the tools of the web. Knowing how to tweet or make a Facebook post is not the same thing as knowing how to build a website and understanding something—even a very little bit—about the structure of how the web works and the techne of it, the communicative aspect of it, the know-how." In all of these situations, these directors are dealing productively and strategically with resistance by treating these moments as an opportunity to correct misconceptions about writing through conversation.

When treated as a productive phenomenon, resistance can also create moments where it is possible to validate *and increase* the disciplinary expertise of instructors who feel underprepared to teach and respond to multimodal composition. One strategy for initiating this process, according to the director of Program 1, is to have "informal conversations with faculty and say, 'Okay, tell me what you're doing in your class.' I tried to figure out what people are already doing that they just don't really talk about, but they get really jazzed about. *People were already doing multimodality*, but they don't necessarily see it that way. They wouldn't call it that" (emphasis added).

These informal conversations allowed this director to connect to the values (and expertise) that instructors within the program already possess. For example, the director at Program 5 knew that the teaching faculty in that program were

> committed to critical, social change pedagogy. We want to be able to enact social change. To do that, we need to be able to compose with different means. . . . If we want to get students not to blindly trust multimodal media, we need to have them understand how manipulatable it is. . . . I think sometimes it was those critical arguments that were really helpful especially for literary scholars. We're not abandoning media critique. In fact, this [having students compose multimodally] is a better way to get students engaged in media critique and to really understand the ideology underneath the media they're engaging.

In this example, the director strategically connected the values of multimodal composition to values already held by the instructors, validating the expertise associated with them. The strategy of assuming expertise in the teaching faculty is particularly savvy: this same director, in moments of resistance, reminded instructors, "You are a skilled teacher of rhetoric and the goal of this project is ultimately to teach effective, re-flective, rhetorical skills and not to teach particular kinds of production skills." Here, the director framed multimodality in terms of rhetoric, in which the instructors of the program are trained during a summer orientation, rather than in terms of technology. In validating the expertise of the instructors, the director also assumes that those instructors are capable of resituating their values, of participating in multimodal curricular transformation.

Professional development opportunities also provide a way to productively engage resistance and simultaneously increase instructor expertise in disciplinary content. This is not an insignificant problem for writing studies. As I mentioned in the first chapter of this book, we do face a unique and complex situation: not only are those teaching composition likely to be least valued by the institution (graduate students, part-time lecturers, etc.), those individuals often possess little to no expertise in the field. Per Elizabeth Wardle and Blake Scott (2015), "Most fields would see graduate training in the field as a necessary qualification for teaching the field's scholarship in upper-division and first-year courses; Rhetoric and Composition is unlike most other fields" (p. 73). In making this observation, Wardle and Scott argue that "the professional faculty who participate in the curriculum design, program creation, advising, and so on, should have shared expertise as well as shared goals and values. While NTTF faculty who teach first-year composition are certainly committed to teaching and have expertise in other areas (creative writing or literature, for example) they often do not have traditionally demonstrable qualifications as scholars in Rhetoric and Composition" (p. 75). The authors go on to describe a cultural shift that took place in their program, and part of that shift involved professional development meetings that helped instructors working in the program cultivate and sustain interactional expertise, which is when an individual has "mastered the language and gained an informed understanding of the specialty without necessarily having contributed to its body of knowledge" (p. 80). In other words, instructors working within a program can develop the expertise necessary to teach multimodal composition even if they are not actively researching and publishing about the concept. It does take sustained and intentional effort, though. This is precisely what several of the case study programs did.

At Program 1, the approach was threefold. First, it involved inviting "compelling speakers to talk on more of a theoretical level. Get people excited and just show them really smart people are doing this work, and it's not a fad. It's not something that is going away. These are literacies that are just as important as what happened in the advent of alphabetic text and the printing press." Second, distribute authority: "I've tried to put people like that in front of our faculty: leaders in the department who are teaching first-year writing and incorporating these things into their class and have them talk about it, because they trust these people more than they trust me." The director of Program 8 agreed, advising, "Figure out how to get buy-in by figuring out who that core group is who will not only be the innovators, who not only have a good sense of the field, not just who have taught writing for 20 years, but those who have a good sense of what Rhetoric and Composition looks like as a field, as a discipline." Those individuals, that director advised, can help create connections to others, bringing them into the cultural shift necessary for multimodal curricular transformation without imposing anything on them. Third, the director of Program 1 mentioned that she has offered "workshops that give really practical assignments and how to assess them." Opportunities like these help teaching faculty understand the theoretical foundations of multimodal curricular transformation and offer practical ways to implement the new curriculum in their own pedagogies and classrooms, thereby increasing their interactional expertise with the discipline and their comfort with multimodality.

The director at Program 10 reiterated this, going into greater detail: "We have these professional development sessions and people learn about different kinds of assignments. When they do, they [instructors in the program] are like 'How does that work? I could do that kind of assignment. Oh, I can do that. Could I borrow your lesson? Can you help me with this?' We had a multimodal fair at the end of the year, and it was really fun. People brought in all kinds of things, and then we've had spots here and there of multimodal stuff." These professional development opportunities create a moment for teaching faculty to see how others who (a) are also anxious about multimodal composition or (b) are already incorporating multimodality in their pedagogies. This model distributes authority and agency to the *whole program* rather than just to the director, which these interviews suggest can decrease resistance to multimodal curricular transformation by encouraging "dialogic collaboration, shared leadership, and diverse sources of authority in policy making, curriculum development, and teacher training" (Goodburn & Leverenz, 1998, p. 280). Program 8's professional development meetings enacted this as well, where members of the teaching faculty introduced the new, transformed multimodal composition curriculum to the rest of the teaching faculty. The director of that program stated that these individuals

had big personalities, were very likeable, very engaging. We put those people up in front. It wasn't always just me. I think that was really important,
because I'm the person in charge, which also means I'm the person who,
you know, who makes sure that TAs are going to class. I have the bad jobs,
too. So, I think it's important to find the people who are trusted, who are
liked, who are engaging, who people know to be good instructors, generally speaking and put them out in front and give them the opportunity to
talk about how they think that this project should be taught.

In utilizing professional development meetings in this way (distributing
authority, providing space for resistance, increasing expertise in multimodal composition, etc.), the culture of the program shifts, inviting
more buy-in to multimodality generally and to multimodal curricular
transformation. The director of Program 5 summarized this strategy in
the following way: "If I tried to pitch it as 'you must do this one thing,' I
would be much less likely to get enthusiastic responses from instructors,
but when they feel like they have the chance to make it their own and
also feel like they have a chance to adopt the pedagogies at their own
pace," there was much more buy-in and less resistance. This illustrates
the importance of creating a culture in which teaching faculty feel valued and heard, something that is necessary for all curricular innovations,
but especially true of multimodal curricular transformation, which can
seem at odds with prior-held conceptions of composition and pedagogical values. In so doing, these directors operate from an ethics of care, in
which Carrie Leverenz (2010) claims that "decisions and actions are thus
motivated not by the protection of individual rights . . . but by the desire
to act in a caring way toward this person or group at this particular time
in this particular context" (p. 9). Treating professional development as
an opportunity for all to lend and expand their expertise does just that
in addition to fostering and supporting curricular transformation.

CONCLUSION

The data collected within these interviews and presented in this chapter
reveal common, ethical, and effective processes and strategies utilized
by directors to bring their programs into multimodal curricular transformation. There are several key findings here that I argue can be utilized
by others if they wish to work toward multimodal curricular transformation in their own programs. First, the most popular and salient motivation for working toward multimodal curricular transformation was
aligning the program's goals and focus with an understanding of FYC
as rhetoric rather than FYC as alphabetic writing. If, as these directors

suggest, the content of FYC is effective communication generally, then multimodal composition allows students to engage the full available means of persuasion. Those who are interested in working toward multimodal curricular transformation might begin by (re)considering the role of rhetoric within their programs' curricula. Additionally, several of these directors mentioned utilizing a co-exigence, a serendipitous moment, to initiate multimodal curricular transformation. For some, this came in the form of financial resources; for others, this was a pre-planned curricular transformation that happened to make space for multimodal composition. The larger takeaway here, though, is for directors interested in multimodal curricular transformation to be ready to move when a moment of opportunity presents itself.

Second, collaboration is an absolutely vital part of multimodal curricular transformation. These directors made sure to mention that these kinds of programmatic changes were not imposed onto the teaching faculty. Rather, the directors utilized various formats (surveys, conversations, professional development meetings, etc.) to provide instructors with the opportunity to have a say in determining the future of the programs in which they work. In so doing, these directors decentered the authority of the program, enacting feminist administrative models. Readers who are interested in bringing about multimodal curricular transformation in their own programs should do the same.

Third, part of collaborating with the teaching faculty within the program involved the collaborative revision of programmatic documents. These documents, like outcomes statements, provide the textual-rhetorical space to articulate and reconsider programmatic values. Readers can use these to define the content of FYC for internal and external audiences, and these interviews suggest that defining FYC as rhetoric rather than as alphabetic writing can carve out a meaningful space for multimodality within curricula. Another effective strategy in revising these documents involved using the WPA OS, a national document informed by disciplinary knowledge, as a source of inventional material and a source of ethos for multimodal curricular transformation. Documents accumulate into cultures, so revising these documents collaboratively with teaching faculty to include multimodal composition can create a very different programmatic culture indeed.

Perhaps the most important findings presented in this chapter related to resistance. These interviews demonstrate quite compellingly that resistance is an inevitable and necessary part of multimodal curricular transformation. This is because resistance can be a starting point for conversations about values and lead to professional development opportunities that can build upon the expertise of the teaching faculty working within the program. Informal conversations with teaching faculty can create moments where rhetorical empathy is possible: directors can hear concerns and anxieties *and* address the misconceptions that might be fueling them. In these case studies, some instructors resisted when they perceived multimodality as outside of the content of composition or at odds with their conception of composition. Where this was the case, the directors discussed how they saw multimodal composition as an extension of rhetoric, as an invocation of the full, available means of persuasion. Rhetoric is a more familiar orientation to composition for these instructors and helped them feel comfortable with successive approximations in implementing a multimodal composition curriculum. Similarly, professional development meetings can productively engage resistance as well. These meetings allow instructors within the program to cultivate their interactional expertise (familiarity with multimodal composition, with rhetoric, with how to respond to and assess multimodal projects, etc.). The most effective examples of this were in programs where instructors working in the program were the ones leading professional development. This simultaneously distributed authority throughout the program *and* helped others build their disciplinary knowledge.

Too often, well-meaning composition program directors perceive resistance from teaching faculty as unproductive or hostile or they believe that it is their job to convert all individuals in the program to their understanding of the role of multimodal composition in FYC. This is not possible, effective, or productive. What will serve us all better is understanding that teacherly identity is closely connected to personal history and conceptions of literacy, both of which are formed long before most folks enter the classroom. In asking instructors to take up multimodal composition, we might be asking them to do something that makes them feel out of control or ignorant. Instead of fighting resistance, we can make the choice to see resistance as an opportunity to discuss values, to make connections, and to strengthen the disciplinary expertise of everyone working within the program. These programs reveal that making that choice is an integral part of multimodal curricular transformation. The next chapter takes up an important finding from this one: the role of outcomes statements in multimodal curricular transformation and how values manifest within (and constrain) programmatic values. Therein, I will explore how outcomes statements can make space for or preclude multimodal composition, tracing the kinds of language we should invoke and the values for which we should strive to craft programmatic documents that lead toward multimodal curricular transformation.

3

OUTCOMES, DEFINITIONS, AND VALUES IN MULTIMODAL CURRICULAR TRANSFORMATION

As evidenced by the findings that I presented in Chapter 2, programmatic documents play a vital role in the dynamic, reflective process of remaking our programs in response to disciplinary advances and the needs of our students. In this chapter, I turn to outcomes statements as one example of these documents, which can be a site of multimodal curricular transformation. The language that we use in our outcomes reveals and reinscribes what it is that we care for in first-year composition, offering definitions, presenting visions, and outlining versions of our curricula. Operating at the intersection of institutions and disciplinary expertise, outcomes provide the textual-rhetorical space for us to (re)negotiate and (re)examine what we want our programs to help students know and do. That kind of value negotiation is an important part of multimodal curricular transformation.

We have paid particular attention to the role of these documents in writing studies. In Chapter 2 I described how the WPA OS came into being: collaboratively crafted through consensus and disciplinary knowledge. The original WPA OS, however, did not account for the effects of different technologies on composing processes. Cynthia L. Selfe and Patricia F. Ericsson (2005) argued that the first iteration focused "largely on traditional writing outcomes," which ignored that "composing practices" can "include a range of other behaviors: reading and composing images and animations; creating multimedia assemblages; combining visual elements, sounds, and language symbols into alternatively organized and presented forms of communication on the Web, in chatrooms, over networks" (p. 32). Years later, Michael Callaway (2013) shared this concern, arguing that "writing" in the WPA OS "appears to mean words, only words and words in a row" (p. 271). He called for revisions to the document that would "present outcomes that emphasize the interconnectedness of writers to writing technologies, encouraging students to critically consider their writerly decisions and online writing

https://doi.org/10.7330/9781646422135.c003

practices, especially in regard to how these online writing decisions and practices influence the interrelation of self-formation and the public sphere," because students "must make tough rhetorical decisions about language, genres of texts and how these genres mesh to produce multimodal texts." (p. 282). In 2008, the statement attempted to address these nuances: What became known as version 2.0 added a "plank" titled Composing in Electronic Environments, which invited students and instructors to consider the ways in which digital technologies can influence and inform the composing process, particularly in the areas of drafting and research. The outcomes in this category read:

- Use electronic environments for drafting, reviewing, revising, editing, and sharing texts;
- locate, evaluate, organize, and use research material collected from electronic sources; and
- understand and exploit the differences in the rhetorical strategies and in the affordances available for both print and electronic composing processes and texts.

These clearly attempt to rectify the gaps in the previous document, demonstrating that the language of the WPA OS can be revised to reflect changing values and rearticulate the content of composition. Local programmatic outcomes, language, and values can be revised in the same way, making multimodal curricular transformation possible in the process.

Indeed, by looking at our outcomes, at the language we utilize to detail our values, we can notice and attend to the ways in which that language prevents us from positioning multimodal composing within the composition curriculum, and alternatively, how we might revise that language to work toward multimodal curricular transformation. In this chapter, I analyze a corpus of outcomes statements—1,353 individual outcomes collected from a total of 82 composition programs—to read across programs, institutions, and outcomes in order to come to an understanding of the language used to signal programmatic values and how that language might preclude or invite multimodal composition and consequently multimodal curricular transformation. I ask, do we (claim to) value multimodal composition at the local level? Do we (claim to) make space for multimodality in our outcomes? And if not, how might we do so? This kind of analysis attempts what Dan Melzer (2014) terms a "panoramic" view, a perspective that "pans wide enough that larger patterns in the landscape are revealed" (p. 3). Typically, the information that we share about what takes place in composition programs comes from isolated examples presented as case studies, descriptions of individual programs, individual classrooms, or individual students. There are several edited collections dedicated to these examples (see, for example: Giberson & Moriarty, 2010; Lee & Khadka, 2018; Khadka & Lee, 2019; Reiff et al., 2015; Siegel Finer & White-Farnham, 2017). These do important work; they render visible the intricacy and nuance of programs in their ecological contexts. However, my goal in this chapter is to use the panorama to gain cross-contextual, data-driven insights about outcomes and values that are flexible enough to be adapted within various institutional types and programmatic structures.

The 1,353 outcomes collected in this corpus depict a continuum of definitions regarding the content of composition programs: on one end of the continuum, there are outcomes that define composition capaciously, including and perhaps requiring multimodal composition; on the other end, there are outcomes that define the content of composition as alphabetic writing only. In tracing this continuum, I present the following findings that will be useful to readers interested in transforming their own curricula and programs:

1. Outcomes that define the content of FYC as solely alphabetic writing prevent us from working toward multimodal curricular transformation while outcomes that define the content of composition more capaciously make transformation possible.

2. This continuum reveals possible alternatives to programs' current outcomes and ways that we can revise our language to work toward transformation.

In the next section, I explain the process of building and coding the corpus before moving into an analysis of the challenges and opportunities presented by the collected outcomes. In my analysis, I begin with multimodal outcomes, illustrating the ways in which those outcomes present competing definitions of multimodality, a hurdle to multimodal curricular transformation, before moving into conventions-, process-, rhetoric-, and critical thinking-based outcomes. This order reflects the frequency with which each type of outcome occurred in the corpus. Within each subsection, I follow the continuum of capaciousness, illustrating how certain outcomes are capacious enough to include multimodal composing while others prevent its inclusion. Thus, readers will leave this chapter with an understanding of how the language we invoke affects curricular content *and* specific examples of outcomes they might consider should they wish to work toward multimodal curricular transformation in their local contexts.

CODING

To locate the outcomes included in the corpus, I used the National Census of Writing, a project that "seeks to provide a data-based landscape of writing instruction at two- and four-year public and not-for-profit institutions of higher education in the United States" (2013) through a comprehensive survey inquiring about institutional regional location, teaching faculty demographics, administrative structure(s), and the curricular content(s) of respondents (National). In its report of the data, the census also includes "Program Profiles," which are published versions of individual survey responses.[1] Ninety-six of the 680 respondents to the 2013 iteration of the survey chose to make their responses publicly available. To locate the programs whose outcomes statements would eventually become the corpus, I reviewed this list of program profiles to determine: (a) if the program had a first-year writing/composition program (instead of a required seminar, for example) and (b) if the program had clearly articulated goals or outcomes (both of these selection criteria are questions asked in the census). Then, I checked each program's website to see if the outcomes were publicly available. If they were not, I sent requests to the directors listed online. This yielded a collection of statements from 82 programs. Of these 82, 46 are doctoral-granting institutions (23 R1s and 23 R2s). The remaining institutions are a mix of private liberal arts colleges and public baccalaureate- or masters-level institutions. Based on these numbers, it is important to note that research-intensive, doctoral-granting institutions are *overrepresented* in the sample. In this regard, the sample is not representative of the field more broadly, nor are the findings statistically generalizable. However, with the funding, resources, and faculty present at those institutions, one would expect these to be model composition programs enacting current trends in disciplinary knowledge. This, as this chapter will demonstrate, was not the case.

Once I located the statements, I sought to "unitize and then categorize" the data (Brice, 2005). I collected statements in a Google Doc, assigned them a program number, and cleared them of identifying information (program name, course title, etc.). I isolated individual outcomes using verb phrases, the smallest meaningful units of what students could be expected to know or do, rather than complete sentences. For example, while "Explore a research subject deeply by identifying important source material about the subject, and engage with

---

1. Respondents must indicate that they are amenable to sharing this information. Otherwise, responses are kept confidential.

that material through analysis, summarization, and visualization," is one sentence, it yields two separate outcomes in my analysis:

1. Explore a research subject deeply by identifying important source material about that subject.
2. Engage with that material through analysis, summarization, and visualization.

Identifying important source material and engaging with that material are two different intellectual activities, and I wanted my analysis to reflect that. This process revealed 1,353 individual outcomes that I could then categorize according to the language used to describe programmatic values. To do this, I utilized a deductive coding method and scheme developed from the WPA OS, which, as I described above, is an articulation of the language used to describe content of composition through different categories: Rhetorical Knowledge, Process, etc. Deductive coding, the application of a predetermined set of codes to the data, is a useful way to approach this set because it helps "focus the coding on those issues that are known to be important in the existing literature, and it is often related to theory testing or theory refinement" (Linneberg & Korsgaard, 2019, p. 264). This deductive approach is able to reveal value frequency, illustrating how often (if at all) certain kinds of outcomes appear, which is especially important in looking for the presence/absence of multimodal composing.

There are limitations to this method of coding, though. Grounded theory approaches to qualitative data now advocate for allowing coding categories to emerge from the data itself (Corbin & Strauss, 2008; Merriam, 2009). Proponents of this approach argue that deductive coding could reduce the nuances of the data set. Consequently, my analysis might not accurately reflect the full complexity of these outcomes. However, the benefits outweighed these limitations because, "while inductive codes have the advantage of being completely loyal to the data, there is a risk of the whole process becoming too complicated and lacking in focus" (Linneberg & Korsgaard, 2019, p. 264). Coding deductively allowed me to gather a panoramic, holistic perspective of what programs within the corpus purport to value by using the language of a national document already in existence. Through this reading, I was able to unpack how those values might make space for or preclude multimodal composing.

I created the coding scheme using the WPA OS as a foundation. The WPA OS was published in 2000, and it included four categories in which students should be proficient by the end of FYC:

1. Rhetorical Knowledge, which pertained to a student's ability to engage the concept of rhetorical situation—responding to an exigence or purpose, catering to the needs of a specific audience, and working with/in the genre(s) appropriate to that situation;

2. Critical Thinking, Reading, and Writing, which emphasized the importance of reading *and* writing in processes of inquiry, research, analysis, and knowledge-making;

3. Processes, which addressed the necessity of multiple drafts and feedback in the completion of composing tasks; and

4. Knowledge of Conventions, which promoted the importance of grammar, spelling, and formatting, including citation practices.

However, as I mentioned earlier, the first version did not account for the possibility of students composing multimodally. The third and most recent version of the statement, released in the summer of 2014, articulates an altogether different version of FYC because "the consensus was that the content of the writing assumed by the statement was becoming underrepresented" (Dryer et al., 2014, p. 136). According to Carrie Leverenz (2016), Statement 3.0 "constitutes a turn away from the original, which had focused unapologetically on traditional academic writing and relegated digital technology to a brief addendum" (pp. 33–34). Indeed, she states, the revised outcomes in Statement 3.0 "offer us an opportunity to rethink the assumption that composition courses serve primarily to prepare students for writing in school" (p. 34). The new statement defines composition more broadly, as "complex writing processes that are increasingly reliant on digital technologies" and acknowledges that "writers also attend to elements of design, incorporating images and graphical elements into texts intended for screens as well as printed pages. Writers' composing activities have always been shaped by the technologies available to them, and digital technologies are changing writers' relationships to their texts and audiences in evolving ways" (Council of Writing Program Administrators). Consequently, Statement 3.0 does not prescribe alphabetic writing as the sole means by which students can accomplish its outcomes, detailing a more capacious vision for and definition of composition. The new statement contains the following categories:

1. Rhetorical Knowledge, defined by the document as "the ability to analyze contexts and audiences and then to act on that analysis in comprehending and creating texts. Rhetorical knowledge is the basis of composing. Writers develop rhetorical knowledge by negotiating purpose, audience, context, and conventions as they compose a variety of texts for different situations";

2. Critical Thinking, Reading, and Composing, defined as "the ability to analyze, synthesize, interpret, and evaluate ideas, information, situations, and texts";

3. Processes, meaning the "multiple strategies, or composing processes, [composers use] to conceptualize, develop, and finalize projects"; and

4. Knowledge of Conventions, now expanded to include "such things as mechanics, usage, spelling, and citation practices. But they also influence content, style, organization, graphics, and document design." (CWPA, 2014)

These changes inform the coding scheme that I utilized to analyze the corpus of statements that I present in this chapter. More specifically, my coding scheme was a hybrid synthesis of Statements 2.0 and 3.0. For example, whereas Statement 3.0 includes multimodal composition consistently and interconnectedly throughout all categories in the document, I made multimodality its own category to highlight the presence/absence of multimodal outcomes. The resulting coding scheme contained five different categories:

- The first category is *Rhetoric and Rhetorical Knowledge.* This code was selected for outcomes that included words and phrases like writing/composing for various purposes and audiences, responding to a variety of rhetorical situations, and working in multiple genres.
- The second category is *Processes,* which, like WPA OS 2.0 and 3.0, accounts for the iterative, chronological, and social production of texts. If an outcome included terms like drafting, revision, feedback, or collaboration, it was coded as Processes. This category also included topics like reflection and metacognition, which, according to the WPA OS, are vital parts of composing/writing processes.
- The third category is *Knowledge of Conventions:* outcomes in this category value the rules and guidelines associated with texts, particularly as they pertain to correctness and appropriateness. Words and phrases in the outcomes that signified this category included grammar, citation, documentation, mechanics, and the common format of texts.
- The fourth category is *Multimodality.* This category was intentionally capacious with the intent of revealing just how present or absent multimodality is in the values of the composition programs included in this corpus. For example, this category included digital and technological literacy, understanding and making use of the capacities of different composing environments, and composing texts made of multiple modes, but it also included simply using modes beyond the written word (like speeches, classroom discussion, adding an image to an essay, etc.).
- The fifth category is *Critical Thinking and Writing.* This code focused on the critical interpretation of texts for research processes

(synthesizing, evaluating, and interpreting ideas), the analysis of texts through various lenses (like literary theory), information literacy and information-seeking behavior, and writing to learn.

Through a generous grant from the Department of English Language and Literature at Eastern Michigan University, I was able to employ research assistants to code statements independent of my own coding. Throughout the process, there were four different research assistants, but two of those completed 80% of the coding. After each statement was coded twice (once by me and once by one of the research assistants), I compared them for discrepancies. When coding discrepancies occurred, the research assistant and I discussed the difference until we reached consensus, modify the coding scheme appropriately, and review the statements we had already coded. Thus, we utilized what Peter Smagorinsky (2008) terms "collaborative coding," in which a pair or team of researchers work collaboratively throughout the entire research process (data collection, development of coding scheme, analysis of data, writing up the results, etc.) to ensure the reliability of the data. Smagorinsky calls into question the traditional belief that "agreement equals reliability" (p. 401), arguing that, in a typical intercoder-reliability scenario, one researcher crafts a coding scheme and codes all of the data before working with a second researcher who independently codes a sample of the same data. If there is "an agreement level of at least 80%" (p. 401), then the application of the coding scheme to the data is said to be reliable. While such a methodology does allow for consistent coding, it also assumes that the data collected and analyzed are fixed entities, that they would be coded the same regardless of the researcher. I do not take this approach to data, understanding that different researchers and different approaches might yield different interpretations. Utilizing collaborative coding ensured rigorous and cooperative data analysis, something I find altogether more important than reliability.

Finally, I should note that generalizability is not the goal of what I present here. My data set does not lend itself to being generalizable: I only collected 82 statements. Melzer (2014) acknowledges this as a limitation for his own study. While he collected over 2,000 assignments from 100 institutions, his findings were not generalizable. He notes that, due to the number of postsecondary institutions in the United States, "a researcher would need to collect writing assignments from approximately *350 institutions*" to reach generalizable conclusions (p. 7, emphasis added). However, even with this limitation, Melzer's data are able to "tell a complex story of college writing" by reading patterns across the sample (p. 5). Thus, my findings here are a snapshot of the panorama, a moment in time for the composition programs represented by the census, but that snapshot, as I will illustrate below, reveals key insights about the language utilized in outcomes statements and how that language can make space for or preclude multimodal composition and multimodal curricular transformation.

RESULTS

The corpus reveals that outcomes that necessitate that students work with/in alphabetic writing leave no space for multimodality, whereas outcomes that use more capacious language make multimodal curricular transformation possible. Knowing this information gives program directors and invested stakeholders the power to revise their outcomes and values, thereby working toward multimodal curricular transformation. Overall, Critical Thinking is the most frequently occurring outcome, averaging 5.6 times per statement; Rhetoric is the second, averaging 3.39 times per statement and accounting for 21% of the total corpus; Processes is the third, averaging 3.20 times per statement; Conventions has very similar totals to Processes, appearing an average of 3.18 times per statement as well. Most disappointing—but perhaps least surprising—is that outcomes related to multimodality occur the most infrequently within this corpus (Table 3.1 depicts the totals and averages of different outcomes according to the coding process). Multimodal outcomes averaged .90 per statement, which means there were programs that did not include multimodal composing among their values at all. Indeed, 47 programs within the corpus included zero multimodal outcomes. While I do not want to imply that there should be a minimum number of multimodal outcomes included within each program or statement, I do want to reiterate that *just over half* of the programs within the corpus do not include outcomes related to multimodality.

As a point of comparison, when WPA OS 3.0 is run through the coding scheme, it reveals the following totals:

Rhetoric: 4
Conventions: 5
Processes: 5
Multimodality: 3
Critical Thinking: 5
Total Outcomes: 22

These frequencies are fairly balanced, and there are outcomes that specifically value multimodal composition. The comparison between the

Table 3.1. Total corpus data

	Avg. Per Statement	Corpus Total	% of Corpus Total
Rhetoric	3.39	282	21%
Conventions	3.18	264	19.5%
Processes	3.20	266	19.6%
Multimodality	0.90	75	5.5%
Critical Thinking	5.61	466	34.4%
TOTALS	16.30	1,353	100%

WPA OS and the corpus totals reveals that there is still work to be done in aligning the published scholarship of the discipline with the work of local programs, because many of these programs do not have a place for multimodality in their curricula, at least officially. In what follows, I will trace each category of outcome (from least to most frequent), uncovering how the language utilized in those categories precludes/includes multimodal composing and how we might revise those definitions to work toward multimodal curricular transformation.

Multimodality

This corpus reinforces my previous finding that we do not (yet) present a consistent definition of multimodality to students (i.e., what work multimodal composition asks students to perform). As I mentioned in Chapter 1, in a previous article I isolated four types of multimodal outcomes: (a) multimodality as the simple addition of another mode on top of writing curricula (typically public speaking or discussion); (b) multimodality as visual rhetoric (prescribing that image be the mode through which students communicate); (c) multimodality as digital or technological literacy; and (d) multimodality as material-rhetorical flexibility, making use of the full available means of communication appropriate for the purpose and situation (Bearden, 2019a). This fourth category most closely resembles the definition of multimodality outlined in contemporary scholarship: not the mere inclusion of digital technology, but an attempt to cultivate in students a knowledge of the limitations and affordances of different composing materials, which allows them to make informed choices in their composing processes. To be sure, outcomes that fall within this fourth category were present in the corpus. However, the other three categories were as well, which suggests that those who are interested in working toward multimodal curricular transformation ought to be mindful of the version of multimodality that they invoke in their documents and present to students.

Multimodality as Presentation/Delivery

Some outcomes could technically be coded as "multimodal" for adding more modes to the curriculum, asking students to do something other than write. However, rather than asking students to theorize the possibilities of multiple modes or to use multimodal composing to achieve rhetorical purposes, these outcomes mostly required that students participate in discussion or give presentations. Some of these outcomes included:

- Deliver well-rehearsed and polished presentations, meeting time, content, and interactive requirements (Program 23).
- Present their work to an academic audience both orally and in writing (Program 49).
- Enhance message through dynamic vocal and physical elements (Program 76).

Here, multimodality is important only insofar as it helps students deliver oral presentations, which is only one kind of communication. Outcomes like these do not engage students in the work of theorizing meaning-making potentialities, which can strengthen their rhetorical practice. In the work of multimodal curricular transformation, programs will want to move away from outcomes like these, which present a very limited understanding of multimodal composition.

Visual Rhetoric

A second, similarly sized cluster conflates multimodality with visual rhetoric, which does expand the content of composition beyond alphabetic writing, but prescribes that students work with the visual, an approach that might have ableist implications and limit students' rhetorical possibilities. For example, these kinds of outcomes ask students to:

- Collect, analyze, and organize research information in verbally and visually compelling ways (Program 18).
- Understand how popular, academic, and/or technical ideas can be communicated visually (Program 64).
- Use visual aids that are effective and compelling (Program 76).

The first outcome in this list implicitly argues that the verbal and the visual are the only two ways of communicating information or are the only acceptable ways to communicate information within the academy. Outcomes like this one ignore the larger repertoire of meaning-making possibilities available to students and instructors. A more capacious and less prescriptive outcome would remove those qualifiers and require only that students present information in compelling ways, regardless of mode and medium. The other two outcomes require that students work within the visual, but in so doing, they subordinate the visual to the verbal: Communicating ideas visually supposes that ideas are constructed verbally before being translated into the visual, and the term "visual aids" suggests that there is a more substantive verbal text doing more intensive meaning-making. These outcomes reinforce the position of power that print, alphabetic writing continues to have within the academy. If we are truly to achieve multimodal curricular transformation, we must ensure that the language utilized to manifest our values does not continue to position multimodal composing as ancillary or require visual rhetoric be the only way in which students can compose multimodally.

Additionally, despite its popularity within writing studies, visual rhetoric (and its study) operates from the ableist assumption that all people can access the visual or access it in the same way. This is a problem with multimodal theory in general. Per Yergeau et al. (2013), "multimodality as it is commonly used implies an ableist understanding of the human composer." This is a major issue for those of us who teach composition and work in composition programs because, "for educators, it is ethically questionable to practice pedagogies and construct spaces that categorically exclude entire classes of people. We need to pay attention to the teaching of composition through the lens of disability studies to remind ourselves of just how much our profession has to learn, and just how much we have been content to ignore. In this important sense, disability studies reminds compositionists that our programs, curricula, and classes are designed to work for only some bodies, not for all bodies" ("Over there"). In their current iterations, these kinds of outcomes lead to what Yergeau et al. call "multimodal inhospitality," which "occurs when the design and production of multimodal texts and environments persistently ignore access except as a retrofit. Retrofits are problematic because they tend to be added on only after complaints are lodged *and* determined to be legitimate" ("Modality," emphasis original). In the process(es) of multimodal curricular transformation, we must be mindful of the (in)hospitality of our outcomes and the version of (multimodal) composition that we present to students.

Multimodality as Digital Literacy

There were several multimodal outcomes that ask students to cultivate digital literacy. Outcomes like these expect students to:

- Gain competence in using computer technology in the writing process (Program 13).

- Use a range of available technologies to support their reading, writing, and thinking, including but not limited to email, word-processing, and database searching (Program 16).

- Use electronic environments for drafting, reviewing, revising, editing, and sharing texts (Program 22).

- Be provided with instruction on various forms of electronic media (e.g., Blackboard, internet sources, word processing tools, etc.) and use such technologies to create, revise, and/or distribute their writing (Program 63).

- Develop technological literacies as they pertain to researching and composing in the twenty-first century (Program 68).

To be clear, digital literacy is important in the twenty-first century because not only has digital communication proliferated outside of the academy, but "in less than thirty years digital technology has become a part of higher education" and "in that short time, computer technologies have literally electrified writing instruction. . . . Even if we teach in traditional classrooms, it is difficult to imagine writing instruction without computer technology and impossible to ignore its impact on literacy" (Sidler et al., 2008, p. 2). We cannot ignore the times. However, these kinds of outcomes place the focus on *using* technology in service of (alphabetic) writing. For example, in the outcome from Program 13, students are not engaging computer technology critically to determine its rhetorical potentialities. Rather, they are gaining competence in service of "the writing process," which in this program involves "express[ing] your ideas with clarity and with effective syntax and punctuation," a very specific kind of alphabetic writing. Similarly, in Program 63, students are not considering the implications of their rhetorical choices with/in "electronic media"—they are using those media to "develop polished essays."

So, while these outcomes are indeed important for the current moment, the language utilized therein continues to privilege alphabetic writing, limiting the kinds of composing students are asked to do. In some programs, these were the only multimodal outcomes. It is possible, however, to craft digital literacy outcomes that also cultivate material-rhetorical flexibility. For example, Program 14 includes an outcome that reads, "You will have composed using digital technologies, gaining awareness of the possibilities and constraints of electronic environments." While this does prescribe that students work with electronic-digital tools, it also encourages students to learn the "possibilities and constraints" of different materials. In this program, students engage those differences rather than merely using tools to perform alphabetic writing. If composition programs only have digital-multimodal outcomes, I argue that Program 14's outcome provides a model that aligns with current trends in writing studies and helps us work toward multimodal curricular transformation.

Multimodality as Capacious Composing

The fourth category of multimodal outcomes presents a capacious version of multimodality and encourages rhetorical-material flexibility in students. These outcomes, I argue, align most closely with the version of multimodality presented in contemporary scholarship. There were three frequently recurring outcomes that fell into this fourth category. They were:

- Understand and use a variety of technologies to address a range of audiences (Programs 15, 17, 21, 22, 24, 33, 41, 46, 65 80, 82).
- Match the capacities of different environments (e.g., print and electronic) to varying rhetorical situations (Programs 15, 17, 21, 24, 33, 41, 46, 80, 82).
- Adapt composing processes for a variety of technologies and modalities (Programs 15, 17, 21, 33, 41, 46, 80, 82).

The first one encourages flexibility, adaptability, and plurality by using the terms "variety" and "range" without prescribing the specific technologies or audiences with which students can work. The second invites students to be aware of and employ the affordances of different materials for various purposes. The third outcome puts rhetorical knowledge, material knowledge, and material-rhetorical flexibility into the practice of "process." All three assist students in cultivating the knowledge necessary to engage multimodal composition.

These three outcomes are particularly interesting and important because they are copied verbatim from WPA OS 3.0. In 2013, Emily Isaacs and Melinda Knight made the argument that perhaps the WPA OS as a document had not had the impact that the field would have liked it to have.[2] This was disappointing because at the time of that chapter's publication, the 2008 WPA OS technology plank had been in circulation for years. The data that I presented in my own prior study suggested that the WPA OS had indeed informed the outcomes that I examined but that those outcomes did not (yet) reflect the revisions

---

2. They present two findings relevant to this study: (a) "the WPA OS has not been broadly adopted or even adapted by our nation's colleges and universities" (p. 300) and (b) "the fifth area of the WPA OS, 'composing in electronic environments,' has had virtually no impact at all" (p. 301).

released in WPA OS 3.0 (Bearden, 2019a). The difference in Isaacs and Knight's findings and my own suggests that documents like the WPA OS might take a while to work their way into local contexts, but they do eventually achieve some influence. Thus, while multimodality does not occur very frequently *overall*, these outcomes from WPA OS 3.0 have found their way into about 10% of programs within the corpus. In a few years, there may be many more programs/outcomes that value multimodality, especially because these programs are mostly housed in research-intensive, doctoral-granting institutions that are more likely to have the resources (financial and personnel) to craft current, up-to-date composition programs. The success of WPA OS 3.0 in this corpus suggests that it might be a beneficial starting point for programs looking for models of outcomes that can help work toward multimodal curricular transformation.

Another possible starting point for crafting multimodal outcomes that reflect contemporary scholarship in multimodal theory is an attention to genre. There were many outcomes within the fourth category of multimodality that asked students to demonstrate genre awareness and flexibility as a part of multimodal composition, which embraces the complexity of multimodal composition presented in scholarship. Some examples of these outcomes included:

- Adapt an argument to a variety of genres and media to suit different audiences and purposes (Program 9).
- Use a variety of technologies, media and/or genres to address a range of audiences (Program 69).
- Demonstrate how to negotiate variations in conventions by genre, from print-based compositions to multi-modal compositions (Program 48).
- Recognize the affordances of a variety of genres, media, platforms, and technologies (Program 61).

Each of these emphasizes multiplicity. The goal of such outcomes is to cultivate an awareness of how the varying semiotic materials that make up modes, media, and technologies change the kinds of texts that can be created. The language utilized in these outcomes emphasizes the important intersection between rhetorical genre studies and multimodal theory. For Bawarshi and Reiff (2010), the study of genre "calls for recognizing how formal features, rather than being arbitrary, are connected to social purposes and ways of being" (p. 4). An understanding of the formal features of texts benefits from understanding the social implications of those features. Similarly, Gunther Kress (2010) writes that "genre addresses the semiotic emergence of social organization, practices and interactions. It names and 'realizes' knowledge of the world as social action and interaction. . . . It comes through participation in events formed of such actions experienced as recognizable practices" (p. 113). Later, he states, "Genre mediates between the social and semiotic: it points to social organization and points to semiotic arrangements which realize these" (p. 116). Genre, in these outcomes and within multimodal composition, is a way of framing semiotic material to achieve certain social actions, making it just as important as mode, medium, platform, and technology in meaning-making and communication. In other words, by attending to genre, these outcomes make space for (and account for the complexity of) multimodality in composition curricula.

To summarize, examining the varying kinds of multimodal outcomes in this corpus reveals three useful takeaways for those interested in pursuing multimodal curricular transformation. First, the WPA OS does appear to have influenced these programs: There were at least three specific outcomes coded as "multimodal" that were directly taken from the WPA OS 3.0 and incorporated into multiple programs. Those recently revised outcomes are indeed (slowly) having an effect on local programs, and thus we would do well to continue to value multimodal composition in our disciplinary documents *and* use those documents as models for our local programs. Second, within this corpus, programs struggle to delineate collectively a consistent version of multimodality to students: spoken presentations, technological literacy, visual rhetoric, and multimodal *composing* are all possibilities other than writing in which students can engage. However, if we are to follow the lead of multimodal scholarship, we should strive toward valuing the robustness of multimodal composing: understanding the limitations and affordances of different resources (modes, media, genres, etc.) and employing those in a rhetorically strategic manner according to purpose, audience, etc. Finally, multimodality continues to be undervalued in our programs compared to its representation in our scholarship. As I will suggest in the remainder of this chapter, this is, in part, because the language utilized by programs to articulate their values can be at odds with multimodal composing. To be clear, I am not arguing that all outcomes must make space/account for multimodality. I do, however, want to illustrate that a good number of our outcomes, in which we articulate our values and beliefs about composing, require that students work with alphabetic writing only. If we wish to work toward multimodal curricular transformation, we must interrogate the assumptions underlying our outcomes and revise accordingly.

Conventions

The full definition of Conventions, per WPA OS 3.0, is "the formal rules and informal guidelines that define genres, and in so doing, shape readers' and writers' perceptions of correctness or appropriateness. Most obviously, conventions govern such things as mechanics, usage, spelling, and citation practices. But they also influence content, style, organization, graphics, and document design" (Council of Writing Program Administrators). Yet, while the WPA OS and other scholars (see Halbritter, 2013, for example) account for more holistic rhetorical considerations in the shape and structure of (multimodal) texts, in practice, this category can be the most restrictive. Indeed, a majority of the outcomes in this corpus that were coded as Conventions privileged mechanics, spelling, and citation practices, all of which prescribe a certain kind of academic, alphabetic writing. Overall, there were 259 outcomes coded as "Conventions" within this sample. These occurred an average of 3.16 times per statement, and 19.5% of the total outcomes were related to conventions. While there were certain outcomes that make space for multimodality by attending to the rhetorical structures of texts depending on the rhetorical situation, just over half of these (133 outcomes) are inhibitive of multimodal curricular transformation and necessitate (re)examination because of the ways in which they (continue to) privilege alphabetic writing.

Challenges

The most restrictive Conventions-based outcomes value "correct" grammar and usage in terms of alphabetic writing. If outcomes signal and reinforce the values of programs, then these outcomes define the work of the composition program as grammatically correct writing, an approach to composing that both precludes multimodal composing and perpetuates racist institutional practices. A few examples from within this category read:

- Use correct syntax, grammar, and mechanics (Program 79).
- Write grammatical sentences (Program 10).
- Produce writing that is free of grammatical and mechanical errors that inhibit or interfere with the reader's understanding (Program 45).
- Includes few errors in grammar, punctuation, and usage (Program 76).

In focusing on the form of writing—specifically, achieving the "correct" form—such programs impose standards upon students under the guise of helping those students produce communication that does not inhibit the process of meaning-making between readers and writers. Many of the outcomes in this category require that students exhibit standard American English (SAE) as a norm:

- Apply the conventions of standard edited American English (Program 60).
- Use syntactically fluent and lexically appropriate language that adheres to the conventions of Standard Written English to develop and support ideas (Program 56).
- Produce standard edited American English (Program 7).
- Follow conventions of Standard Edited English (Program 47).

There are several issues with these outcomes and the values they manifest. By requiring that students work within the medium of print, SAE writing, and requiring *how* they work within that medium, outcomes like these leave no space for multimodal composition, something that those of us who work within these programs should address if we want to work toward multimodal curricular transformation. More important, they operate under the assumption that American English can actually be standard, ignoring the fact that regional dialects affect and influence meaning-making processes and assuming that all parts of the academy communicate using the same English.

The larger issue here, though, is the epistemological violence at work in forcing students to learn to use SAE and/or to assess students according to SAE's expectations. In 1974, the Students' Rights to their Own Language position statement argued that there is no inherent prestige or value in SAE. In holding students to the standards of SAE, we invalidate their personal dialects, which is a significant issue "since dialect is not separate from culture, but an intrinsic part of it, accepting a new dialect means accepting a new culture; rejecting one's native dialect is to some extent a rejection of one's culture" (CCCC, 2014). Indeed, SAE is more of an indication of cultural position (or privilege) than writerly aptitude. Geneva Smitherman (1999) writes that "most of these students [who entered the university in the 1960s and 1970s], however bright, did not have command of the grammar and conventions of academic discourse/'standard English.' Yet they often had other communicative strengths—creative ideas, logical and persuasive reasoning powers, innovative ways of talking about the ordinary and mundane" (p. 359). The statement on students' rights was developed as a way to navigate this tension. Further, the CCCC Special Committee on Composing a Statement on Anti-Black Racism and Black Linguistic Justice addressed this in a document released in the summer of 2020, demanding that "teachers and researchers acknowledge that socially constructed terms such as *academic language* and *standard English* are false and entrenched in notions of white supremacy and whiteness that contribute to anti-Black linguistic racism" ("This ain't," emphasis original). Such statements are necessary because racism via the imposition of SAE persists. Asao Inoue (2015), for example, states that "racism in schools and college writing courses is still pervasive because most if not all writing courses, including my own in the past, promote or value first a local [SAE] and a dominant white discourse" (p. 14), and within this system, students of color "are often hurt by conventional writing assessment that uncritically uses a dominant discourse" (p. 16). Per Staci Perryman-Clark (2016), this is because "decisions about writing assessment are rooted in racial and linguistic identity; the consequences for many writing assessment decisions are often reflective of the judgments made about who does and does not deserve opportunities for success, opportunities historically denied to students of color and linguistically diverse writers. Put simply, assessment creates or denies opportunity structures" (p. 206). Thus, not only do these outcomes do our students a disservice, but they also perpetuate racist institutional practices.

In moving our values and outcomes away from SAE, we can simultaneously work against these racist systems and work toward multimodal curricular transformation. The culmination of a pedagogy of multiliteracies, is what the New London Group terms transformed practice, "in which students transfer and re-create Designs of meaning from one context to another" using necessarily multimodal means (Cope & Kalantzis, 2000, p. 31), which makes them more effective communicators in a global-digital world. That kind of cross-cultural communication and negotiation resists the supremacy of SAE; being proficient in only one way of communicating is simply not enough for communicators in the twenty-first century. Multimodal curricular transformation, because it encourages students to cultivate material-rhetorical flexibility and the ability to communicate with multiple audiences, provides us a way to work against the fiction that Horner et al. (2011) describe as a "linguistically homogeneous situation: one where writers, speakers, and readers are expected to use Standard English or Edited American English—imagined ideally as uniform—to the exclusion of other languages and language variations" (p. 304). In other words, we can reject and challenge racist institutional practices by accepting and validating, in our outcomes and in our pedagogical practices, ways of communicating outside SAE alphabetic writing.

Opportunities

While the outcomes detailed above were the majority of those coded within this cluster, there were outcomes that were capacious enough to allow for multimodal composing. For example, a few of those that did not prescribe (a certain kind of) alphabetic writing included:

- Provide an understanding of the conventions of multimodal composition that comprise developing communication in the twenty-first century (Program 9).
- Apply conventions of format, design, and structure appropriate to the rhetorical situation (Program 66).
- Use conventions of format and structure appropriate to the rhetorical situation (Program 70).
- Present information in a succinct, smooth, logical manner (Program 76).

These are rhetoric-based outcomes that can foster multimodality. They do not prescribe the materials, media, or modes in which students work. Rather, they focus instead on students making material-rhetorical-structural choices that are appropriate to the given rhetorical situation. These kinds of outcomes make multimodal curricular transformation possible by strengthening students' understandings of rhetoric, thereby making them more effective and adroit composers.

PROCESS

Outcomes coded as "Process" reinforce key findings that I have outlined thus far, namely that the WPA OS is slowly impacting the work of local programs and that outcomes that prescribe alphabetic writing are inhibitive of multimodal curricular transformation. Process-based outcomes appeared an average of 3.18 times per statement, and the 261 outcomes comprised 19.6% of the corpus. To reiterate, the coding scheme that I utilized in this project defined Process as:

- accounting for the fact that composing takes place over time;
- accounting for the social and collaborative aspects of the composing process, including the role of feedback; and
- considering the metacognitive aspects of the composing process, including reflection.

Several outcomes that recurred throughout the corpus are clearly based on and/or developed from the WPA OS. Here are a few examples of those outcomes:

- Develop a writing project through multiple drafts (Programs 15, 17, 21, 33, 41, 45, 80, 82).
- Learn to give and to act on productive feedback to works in progress (Programs 15, 17, 21, 24, 33, 41, 46, 53, 80, 82).
- Experience the collaborative and social aspects of writing processes (Programs 15, 17, 21, 33, 41, 46, 80, 82).
- Develop flexible strategies for reading, drafting, reviewing, collaborating, revising, rewriting, rereading, and editing (Programs 15, 17, 21, 24, 33, 41, 46, 48, 80, 82).
- Reflect on the development of composing practices and how those practices influence their work (Programs 15, 17, 21, 24, 33, 41, 46, 53, 80, 82).

The outcomes in this selection have been taken verbatim from WPA OS 3.0, illustrating that the document can (eventually) influence local programs. Indeed, 9%–12% of the programs included in this study defer to the values articulated in the statement, and this is a much more optimistic number than that presented by Isaacs and Knight in 2013. Thus, while the document might be slow to take effect, it is, for these programs at least, taking effect, a promising finding considering the ways in which WPA OS 3.0 makes room for multimodal composition.

Challenges

However, the language we use to discuss the composing process can preclude multimodality if that language presents alphabetic writing as the only medium in/with which students work. When we invoke the term "writing" in our outcomes, it does not always mean the capacious definition of writing presented in scholarship and in our professional documents, like the current iteration of the WPA OS. This is especially important to recognize because the vocabulary that we use in value articulation matters, especially to external audiences who might not share our beliefs. These outcomes are communicating to those audiences, through the language of process, that composition is alphabetic writing:

- Through the practice of varied writing processes (i.e., reading, drafting, discussion, research, instructor feedback, peer feedback, revision, editing, and proofreading), students will demonstrate a working knowledge of processes for developing polished essays (Program 63).
- Apply revision strategies on all major written texts (Program 60).
- Formulate a coherent writing plan (Program 62).
- Use the writing process—prewriting, writing, drafting, revising, and editing—to write unified and coherent essays (Program 37).
- Revise and edit multiple drafts to produce writing that is well-organized, mechanically and grammatically sound, and mostly error free (Program 35).

Certain preoccupations present in these outcomes limit the possibility of multimodal composition, specifically the emphasis on a linear composing process, an emphasis on argument-based or essay-based texts only, and attachments to coherence/organization in a way that privileges one kind of composing. Multimodal composing does not share these preoccupations. These outcomes position students as writers and define the content of FYC as producing, responding to, and interacting with alphabetic writing. By prescribing the materials with/through which our students learn, we simultaneously limit their rhetorical possibilities and leave no room for multimodality within the content of FYC. While these outcomes do some good work, emphasizing the importance of revision during the composing process and understanding that pieces of a text work together to present a unified whole, they utilize a language and a vocabulary that perpetuates misconceptions about FYC.

Opportunities

There are also process-based outcomes in this corpus that make room for multimodal composition and the possibility of multimodal curricular transformation, and some programs included within this study are already doing that work by utilizing a vocabulary that does not prescribe alphabetic writing. Some examples of this include:

- Know and be able to use several strategies for revising effectively (Program 70).
- Revise to extend their thinking about a topic, not just to rearrange material or "fix" mechanical errors (Program 4).
- Reflect a recursive composing process across multiple drafts (Program 9).
- Apply concepts and terms from the field of rhetoric/composition to reflect critically on their own composing practices and rhetorical decisions (Program 3).
- Engage in the collaborative and social aspects of composing (Program 34, 66).

The outcomes in this list lend themselves to multimodal composing and curricular transformation by invoking a different vocabulary, opting for "composing practices and rhetorical decisions" rather than "writing situations" or "writing processes." These are the kind of rhetoric-based, flexible outcomes that can make space for multimodality. This is still the work of process, but it does not rely on the language and vocabulary of alphabetic writing. A simple change in language—using "texts" and "composing" instead of "essays" and "edit"—could then communicate internally and externally that the composition program does not only concern itself with alphabetic, page- and print-based writing. We can work toward transformation by returning to and revising the language that we utilize to describe project completion.

RHETORIC

Outcomes were coded as pertaining to rhetoric if they asked students to consider:

- that composing varies across contexts, purposes, and audiences;
- that a knowledge of rhetorical vocabulary can inform the composing process; and
- that genre knowledge informs the composing process as well.

Following this definition, the process of coding revealed 278 "Rhetoric" outcomes in this sample: they occurred an average of 3.39 times per statement and accounted for 21% of the entire corpus, making it the second most frequently occurring outcome (behind Critical Thinking).[3] Like the other clusters within this chapter, there were rhetoric-based outcomes that precluded multimodal composing and others that made space for it, especially those that help students cultivate a rhetorical vocabulary, a metalanguage, that they can utilize to make better, more informed composerly choices.

Challenges

Fortunately, only about 8% of the rhetoric-based outcomes in this corpus are inhibitive multimodal composition because they over-determine the ways in which students compose. For example, several emphasize the importance of students being able to construct (academic) arguments. A few of these outcomes read:

- Students will be able to interpret their research findings in order to produce arguments that matter to specific communities by addressing real-world exigencies (Program 31).
- Create effective and sustainable arguments (Program 45).
- Assert and defend a thesis that argues a position in response to a task or for a purpose (Program 56).
- Produce college-level academic arguments (Program 44).

---

3. This is a key difference between this study and another that I conducted in 2015 (see Bearden, 2019a). In that study, rhetoric-based outcomes were the fourth most frequently occurring kind of outcome. I attribute this change over time to WPA OS 3.0, in which the content of first-year composition is defined capaciously, and rhetoric is the vehicle through which the composing process is theorized. See Processes section for another example of the way in which WPA OS 3.0 impacted the programs that are the focus of the current study.

Emily Isaacs (2018) has written about the prevalence of argumentation as the focus of composition. In her study of state universities, 62% ($n = 65$) "were coded as emphasizing argumentation" (p. 117). In such programs, she writes, "the argumentative essay was listed as either the only genre or one among just a few . . . often suggesting that the argumentative essay is the preferred form" (p. 118). This prevalence leads her to claim that "argument has won the day both in and outside the discipline" (p. 118). While that victory is not felt quite as powerfully in this corpus, it is worth noting because such outcomes might prescribe a very specific kind of alphabetic writing, one that does not allow for the inclusion of multimodality. For example, in Program 45, those "effective and sustainable arguments" are also expected to be produced in "writing that is free of grammatical or mechanical errors." Similarly, in Program 56, students must use "syntactically fluent and lexically appropriate language that adheres to the conventions of Standard Written English." Thus, while it may be the case that not all arguments are made in alphabetical writing, we must be aware of how argument-focused outcomes can lend themselves to a prescriptive form of communication.

The difficulty here is the inextricable connection between the history of rhetoric, which has privileged persuasion and argumentation, and the history of composition, which has privileged persuasive and argumentative texts. As Adam Banks (2015) argues, "the essay is a valuable, even powerful technology that has particular affordances in helping us foster communicative ability, dialogue, and critical thinking. But we have gotten too comfortable relying on those affordances as our writing and communication universe go through not only intense change, but an ever-increasing tempo of change" (p. 273). The persistent presence of outcomes that privilege the essayistic, argument-based way of knowing and communicating functions as an invitation for us to continue reimagining rhetoric (a la Gearhart, 1979; Foss & Griffin, 1995; and Prior et al., 2007). For those who are interested in moving toward curricular transformation by placing multimodality within the content of composition, it is important to be mindful of the version of rhetoric and of argumentation presented to students and how that version might preclude multimodal composing.

Opportunities

The overwhelming majority (over 90%) of the rhetoric-based outcomes in the corpus allow for and invite multimodal composing. They do so because they treat composition as a techne—a craft that can be learned through a knowledge of key terms and concepts (Atwill, 1998). Such outcomes focus on the cultivation of flexibility via rhetorical knowledge and a rhetorical vocabulary/metalanguage without prescribing that alphabetic writing be the vehicle in which students work. For example, one of the ways in which these outcomes ask students to develop and display flexibility is through the concept of rhetorical situation. Rhetorical situations, as the contexts in which rhetoric occurs, require a flexible, adaptive analysis that will lead to effective performances within those contexts. Outcomes that fell within this subcategory included:

- Assess rhetorical situations in order to act within them (Program 26).
- Create texts that respond to a variety of rhetorical situations (purpose, audience, context) (Program 60).
- Develop facility in responding to a variety of situations and contexts calling for purposeful shifts in voice, tone, level of formality, design, medium, and/or structure (Programs 15, 33, 46).
- Develop a repertoire of diverse rhetorical strategies that will enable you to assess and appropriately respond to each assignment's audience and purpose (Program 27).

These acknowledge how composing practices vary across contexts and purposes. Part of being able to negotiate those variances involves the recursive relationship between analysis and performance within rhetorical situations. By using a rhetorical vocabulary—audience, context, purpose, etc.—students can understand the situation at hand and respond effectively. These outcomes value plurality and assume that students will be working in multiple situations. They invite and foster multimodal composition. To reiterate, scholarship in multimodality does not prescribe that students work with only digital texts. Rather, it advocates for students cultivating a metalanguage that they can utilize to theorize the limitations and affordances of various composing tools. Outcomes pertaining to rhetorical situation function similarly. Therefore, programs that wish to work toward multimodal curricular transformation should emphasize the importance of rhetorical situation in composing.

Outcomes that attend to genre knowledge, performance, and flexibility also make space for multimodal composing and multimodal curricular transformation by helping students strengthen their composerly craft without being too prescriptive. I have included "genre" within this category (rather than in Conventions) because genre theory has advanced beyond the notion that genre knowledge is limited only to the common formats of texts. Instead, rhetorical genre studies (RGS) identifies the rhetoricity of genres as the social (inter)actions they make possible (see, for example, Devitt, 1993; Miller, 1984; Giltrow, 2002). In expanding the circumference of analysis from formats to actions, genre-based outcomes make space for multimodal composition as well. For example, some of the outcomes in this subcategory read:

- Demonstrate awareness of the role of genre in the creation and reception of texts (Program 9).
- Learn how to invoke common expectations between writers and readers and how these expectations vary by genre and discipline (Program 24).
- Gain experience reading and composing in several genres to understand how genre conventions shape and are shaped by readers' and writers' practices and purpose. (Programs 15, 17, 21, 24, 33, 41, 42, 46).
- Gain experience negotiating variations in genre conventions (Programs 15, 17, 33, 41, 42).

These outcomes value the ability to negotiate situational-(con)textual variations and make space for multimodal composition by fostering flexibility. This knowledge makes students more effective and adroit composers by fostering flexibility through practice. In so doing, students develop a flexible set of composing strategies that they can utilize regardless of context. These kinds of genre-based outcomes, then, would be useful for programs that wish to work toward multimodal curricular transformation.

CRITICAL THINKING

The coding scheme defined the category of Critical Thinking as:

- focused on the critical interpretation of texts for research processes (synthesizing, evaluating, and interpreting ideas),
- the analysis of texts through various lenses,
- information literacy and information-seeking behavior, and
- writing to learn.

The majority of the outcomes in this corpus were coded as Critical Thinking: 461 in total. This category appeared, on average, more than five times per statement and accounted for 35% of the overall collection. This category, its noticeable frequency, and the values articulated therein raise interesting questions for those of us who participate in the administration, curricular revision, and design of composition programs, particularly as they relate to multimodal curricular transformation. As I will trace here, while these outcomes have the potential to cultivate information literacy and critical reading skills that can strengthen students'

composing practices, some of these inhibit multimodal curricular transformation by using outdated pedagogical approaches and/or prescribing certain kinds of writing and thinking that do not allow students to
engage multimodal composition.

Challenges

Some of these outcomes are tied to outdated approaches to teaching
composition, like utilizing literature as the content of the composition
classroom, which prescribes a certain kind of textual consumption.
While I do not wish to argue that outcomes that focus on the consumption of texts are always inhibitive of multimodal composition, I do want
to acknowledge that these outcomes are tied to a problematic model of
composing. Six programs out of the 82 collected and analyzed for this
study included outcomes that prescribed the study and reading of literature. The assumption here appears to be that if students are exposed
to and/or enjoy reading literature, they will somehow learn to write
more effectively. There were 11 outcomes like these, accounting for 2%
of total Critical Thinking outcomes. Some are designed to foster a love
of literature and reading in students, while others foster critical literary
consumption. Program 2, for example, requires that students "utilize
close reading as a primary skill of *literary analysis*" (emphasis added). As I
mentioned earlier in this chapter, reading to understand rhetorical concepts in action and to develop a rhetorical vocabulary/metalanguage
has direct benefits for students by helping them understand composing
as a series of more- or less-effective choices. Critical, close reading is an
interpretive analytical tool that does have value, but outcomes like these
necessitate that students work with, study, and analyze literature, which
can be prescriptive in approach and inhibitive of multimodal composition. One of program 69's outcomes is that students will "interpret literary texts, such as non-fiction, short stories, poems, songs, and/or films
with a specific focus on theoretical frame," which predetermines the
kinds of analyses that students can perform and the kinds of texts they
can write. Similarly, Program 37 includes an outcome that students will
"analyze the use of literary terms in drama, poetry, and fiction, including
plot, character, theme, point of view, setting, and—for poetry—imagery,
figurative devices, and sounds." Here, the program not only requires
that students work with/in literature but also that students utilize a
predetermined vocabulary to do so. All of this is done, according to
Program 54, in the hopes that students "will acquire a mastery of the
tools of literary analysis and a deeper understanding of how these tools
help unlock the power and relevance of literature," and that they will

"be exposed to imaginative texts that spark their curiosity and foster a life-long love of reading" (Program 54). Missing from these outcomes is an attention to flexibility: literary analysis is one kind of thinking and one kind of composing. To work toward multimodal curricular transformation and more rhetorically informed composition programs, we must move away from these kinds of values and outcomes.

The category of Critical Thinking also included processes of research and the presentation of research. The largest sub-category of outcomes (164 outcomes) under the umbrella of Critical Thinking relates to inquiry and information-seeking behavior. For example:

- Locate and evaluate (for credibility, sufficiency, accuracy, timeliness, bias, and so on) primary and secondary research materials, including journal articles and essays, books, scholarly and professionally established and maintained databases or archives, and informal electronic networks and internet sources (Programs 15, 17, 21, 24, 33, 41, 46, 47, 48, 53, 60, 61, 80, 82).
- Locate, engage with, and integrate evidence into your argument (Program 20).
- Become skilled at locating primary and secondary research from a variety of sources (Program 45).

Once students locate and engage these sources, they are expected to perform source work. One of the most common words to appear in this sub-category was "integrate." Some of these outcomes read very specifically:

- **Integrate** primary and secondary research as appropriate to the rhetorical situation (Program 18).
- Use strategies—such as interpretation, synthesis, response, critique, and design/redesign—to compose texts that **integrate** the writer's ideas with those from appropriate sources (Programs 15, 17, 21, 24, 33, 41, 46, 53, 80, 82).
- **Integrate** their own ideas effectively and ethically with those from rhetorically appropriate sources with appropriate citation conventions (Program 60).
- **Integrate** relevant evidence for the audience, context, and purpose, including reliable documented sources (Program 56).

This kind of synthesis demonstrates an advanced understanding of research, the ways in which texts influence other texts, and the circulation of ideas in specific disciplines. However, the complete statements from which some of these come reveals an overall definition of composing that precludes multimodal composing and is inhibitive of multimodal curricular transformation. Program 6, for example, also expects students to "produce Standard Edited American English." Program 23 defines the kind of writing that students will perform even more specifically: "Develop and support a relevant and informed thesis, or point of view, that is appropriate for its audience, purpose, discipline, and theme." Not least, in Program 79, students are expected to "demonstrate an ability to focus on purpose in a longer written work," which is then assessed through an argumentative research paper. So, while research and inquiry do not always have to lead to a research paper, these outcomes and programs require that they do. Like literary analysis, the research paper is but one kind of composing—a useful kind to be sure, but one where multimodality is likely to be excluded due to the focus on alphabetic writing.

These programs are not unique. Emily Isaacs's work makes it clear that the research paper continues to have a privileged position in the academy—she reports that 91.4% of courses in the sample she collected "included research instruction" (2018, p. 99) and that 85.9% of respondents to her survey "identified the research essay as a required part of the FYC course or sequence of courses, suggesting a trend toward research in support of writing an essay rather than research for the sake of reporting" (p. 99). If students are required to write the research paper as it has been traditionally conceptualized (print, argument-driven, etc.), students might be prevented from engaging in the work of multiliteracies and multimodal composing, which involves the selection of the materials appropriate for the task and then deploying those materials appropriately. The persistent presence and frequency of these kinds of outcomes ask us all to reconsider how research and the research paper manifest within FYC and how both might impede multimodal curricular transformation.

Opportunities

There are, however, outcomes within this category that could be useful for multimodal composing. Unlike the outcomes focused on literary close reading and analysis detailed above, these outcomes invoke critical reading as understanding and following along with effective rhetorical strategies. For example, Program 64 asks students to "read texts with a writerly eye so as to identify and evaluate rhetorical strategies and approaches as potential models for your own writing." Here, the goal is for students to see writing as a series of choices that are made by writers, very similar to rhetorical knowledge and performance discussed elsewhere in this chapter. In this way, students can utilize that theoretical understanding to make more informed and effective choices in their own writing. Similar kinds of outcomes read:

- Identify and evaluate persuasive strategies including logical, ethical, and emotional appeals in written, oral, and visual media (Program 8).
- Use reading strategies in order to identify, analyze, evaluate, and respond to arguments, rhetorical elements, and other genre conventions in college-level texts and other media (Program 30).
- Use a diverse range of texts, attending especially to relationships between assertion and evidence, to patterns of organization, to the interplay between verbal and nonverbal elements and to how these features function for different audiences and situations (Program 48).

In these outcomes, students are reading critically and rhetorically with the goal of making more informed compositional choices as a result of that reading. Indeed, Program 8 follows up by stating that students will be able to "use appropriate logical, ethical, and emotional appeals to adapt language to a specific audience to be persuasive." While this is not the case of all of the outcomes included in the corpus, it does reveal one way in which Critical Thinking outcomes can be shaped and revised to foster multimodal curricular transformation.

There were also several outcomes in this corpus related to social justice and equity, which also provide productive models for outcomes that could foster multimodal curricular transformation. While these are not specifically related to writing knowledge or development, they do belong in the Critical Thinking category because they are similar to an outcome from WPA OS 2.0 that asked students to understand the relationships among language, knowledge, and power. Some of these outcomes focus on the importance of cultural awareness, perhaps as an attempt to foster viewpoint diversity within students. For example, Program 26 has an outcome that states, "Cultivate an attitude of openness toward other perspectives, including response to one's own productions." Others focus on issues of equity: Program 2 asks students to "understand the significance of historically underrepresented perspectives and traditions," and similarly, Program 9 seeks to have students "question existing assumptions about culture and community." In examining these outcomes related to social justice and equity, I initially wondered how they fit within the purview of the composition curriculum. The answer, I believe, appears in some of the other outcomes within this cluster. Program 26, for example, invites students to "revise purposes and approaches in relation to developing cultural knowledge." These outcomes recognize that we do not compose in isolation: we make and share meaning as members of various communities to/for/with members of various communities. To do the important work of speaking across those communities, students must know and understand differences. In so doing, "students will be able to view themselves as engaged citizens within an interconnected and diverse world" (Program 38). These outcomes have an important place in a transformed multimodal composition curriculum. As I mentioned earlier, the goal of a pedagogy of multiliteracies is to foster in students the ability to cross cultures and contexts. According to Kathy Mills (2008), this pedagogy is "equally concerned with the global diversity of languages and cultures and the associated generation of diverse texts" (p. 110). Fostering cultural awareness will make it easier for students to understand the multiple, diverse contexts with which they might be expected to interact. Outcomes like these, because they do not prescribe the medium in which students work, and because they foster the intellectual habits necessary for multiliteracies, would be a valuable addition to a transformed multimodal composition curriculum.

CONCLUSIONS

Programmatic documents provide a textual-rhetorical space for those involved in the administration and delivery of academic programs to renegotiate content and values. As such, they are an excellent starting point for multimodal curricular transformation. In this chapter, I turned to outcomes statements as an illustration of this capability: reading across the outcomes in this corpus raises concerns about the spectrum of language that we utilize to articulate and communicate the content of the first-year composition program. One end of the spectrum contains outcomes that define the content of composition as alphabetic writing, prescribing the medium in which students work and consequently precluding multimodal composing; outcomes on the other end of the spectrum define composing as making and sharing meaning with the full available means of persuasion, which invites (and perhaps requires) multimodal composition. The values manifested by this end of the spectrum, it should be clear, are those that make multimodal curricular transformation possible, allowing us the opportunity to present to students a theoretically robust curriculum informed by cutting-edge scholarship.

We must have a conversation about language and the terms that define us as a discipline. Specifically, I believe we must re-evaluate our uses of compose/composition and write/writing. Some scholars perceive "writing" as a term that is capacious enough to include multimodal composing. Cheryl Ball and Colin Charlton (2015) offer "all writing is multimodal" as a threshold concept in writing studies. In their description of this concept, they write, "there is no such thing as a monomodal text. This assumption is a throwback to the romantic version of writing focused solely on alpha-numeric textual production and analysis" (p. 43). In this way, all writing is multimodal, and writing as a term describing what we do in FYC includes multimodal composing. Similarly, Sidney Dobrin (2011), in outlining a vision for the future of composition studies, eschews the term "composition." Composing, he writes, is "an act that is chained . . . to an understanding of student subjects performing that act (often only as an academic performance). Writing is a phenomenon that requires the attention of intellectual and scholarly inquiry and speculation beyond composition. Writing is more than composition studies" (p. 2). In focusing on the performance of student subjects within composition, Dobrin believes composition studies possesses an "inability to articulate an intellectual focus beyond the training of teachers, an activity set in service of the continued management of student bodies" (p. 18). The study of writing that he proposes includes the study of the complexity and flow of texts within networks of activity. Per Dobrin, writing is more capacious, more rigorous, and more contemporary than composition. L. Lennie Irvin (2009) describes a similar approach in one program's shift in name from First-Year Composition to First-Year Writing. Irvin argues that "the name 'Freshman Composition' still evokes the frame in the minds of students, administrators, and the public that this course is a skills course, focusing on correctness in the mechanics and conventions of writing. However, the term 'First-Year Writing' expresses . . . a broader conception of genres available for a writing course, the significance of inquiry, and the representation of writing as an intellectual practice rather than a mere skill." Within these perspectives, "writing" is the more capacious and generative term. Other scholars opt for "composition." Kathleen Blake Yancey (2004a), for example, has articulated a new composition, one that "includes rhetoric and is about literacy. New composition includes the literacy of print: it adds on to it and brings the notion of practice and activity and circulation and media and screen and networking to our conceptions of process" (p. 320). This is strikingly similar to the definition of composition presented in WPA OS 3.0. Even though the document states that composition "refers broadly to complex writing processes that are increasingly reliant on the use of digital technologies," it does go on to say that "writers also attend to elements of design, incorporating images and graphical elements into texts intended for screens as well as printed pages. Writers' composing activities have always been shaped by the technologies available to them, and digital technologies are changing writers' relationships to their texts and audiences in evolving ways" (CWPA, 2014).

These examples reveal and reinforce what is a central issue within this corpus: Our published works, a la Dobrin, WPA OS 3.0, etc., reveal that we possess and operate from a robust conceptualization of writing as more than just alphabetic literacy and that includes the content of the first-year composition program. However, the outcomes contained in this chapter reveal that in local programs, "writing" continues to mean, invoke, and privilege alphabetic writing. Dobrin, Ball, Charlton, and Irvin's idea of writing is not the writing that is presented to students. We cannot assume that our definitions and our terms are shared, and we must acknowledge this disconnect between our published works, which are by necessity cutting-edge and current, and composition programs, which (can) remain fairly conservative in the version of composition that they present to students. In acknowledging this disconnect, we can see that there is work that needs to be done.

Thankfully, my analysis in this chapter reveals a way forward for those who are interested in remedying this disconnect and working toward multimodal curricular transformation, which I will summarize here. Overall, there is language that we might avoid, like "essay" and "paper," because these imply a certain kind of alphabetic writing that precludes multimodal composing. "Composing" and "texts" would serve us better, their flexibility making space for multimodality even if they do not require that students compose multimodally. Additionally, programs would do well to consider adopting some or part of the WPA OS 3.0, which defines the content of FYC capaciously *and* helps local programs align their values and curricula with national best practices. Part of those best practices include ways to categorize the various parts of FYC curricula. I traced this using a coding scheme that helped me label outcomes as Multimodality, Conventions, Processes, Rhetoric, and Critical Thinking, each of which has different lessons to teach us in the effort toward multimodal curricular transformation:

1. **Multimodality.** We must strive to present a consistent version of multimodality to students. Digital literacy, visual rhetoric, face-to-face presentations, and communication are all important, but multimodal outcomes do their best work when they ask students to consider the rhetorical potentialities of different materials *and then* engage those potentialities in practice.

2. **Conventions.** These kinds of outcomes can be particularly problematic for FYC programs working toward multimodal curricular transformation because the application of Conventions can lead to an emphasis on "correct" SAE. In other words, these outcomes can prescribe a kind of academic writing that participates in racist institutional structures. However, Conventions outcomes can foster multimodal composition

and deeper compositional understanding by emphasizing that textual structures depend on rhetorical situations and by not prescribing the materials with/in which students work.

3. **Processes.** Outcomes under this category should foster metacognition and reflection as ways to implement more effective composerly choices and should encourage in students the ability to conceptualize a project as a series of tasks without using the language of essays, papers, and drafts, which can prohibit students from working with different kinds of materials.

4. **Rhetoric.** This is perhaps the most influential category of outcome because, through a rhetorical knowledge, students can cultivate a meta-language that they can use to theorize the composing process across contexts, situations, purposes, and audiences. These outcomes should focus less on crafting persuasive academic arguments and more on learning rhetorical concepts (like rhetorical situation) and working with whatever materials and approaches might be the most effective for the given task.

5. **Critical Thinking.** Critical reading, which is part of critical thinking, benefits students if it helps them gain an understanding of the way in which texts function. Reading for patterns and strategies to help them develop their composerly repertoire, rather than reading for the sake of reading literature, can help students cultivate the metalanguage necessary to engage rhetoric and multimodal composition. Additionally, while research and inquiry are useful intellectual activities for students in the academy, pairing those activities with a traditional, print, argument-driven research paper limits students' possibilities by precluding the multimodal. Not least, programs should not shy away from issues related to social justice. These outcomes foster cross-cultural understanding and empathy, valuable parts of the pedagogy of multi-literacies. The goal of expanding the kinds of texts that students create is to expand the kinds of people to whom they can speak, and these outcomes make that possible.

It is my hope that readers will be able to take these findings to their local contexts, sharing them with their peers, initiating conversations about the content of composition and how that content must necessarily include multimodal composition if we are to help our students be effective citizens in a global-digital world. Those conversations about content and values, I believe, are the first steps in multimodal curricular transformation. In the following chapter, I examine how these values radiate out from these documents into the assignments delivered to students, exploring how the case study programs that I discussed in Chapter 2 present multimodality to their students.

4

MANIFESTATIONS OF MULTIMODAL CURRICULAR TRANSFORMATION

In Chapter 2 of this book, I detailed the processes by which 10 case study programs initiated multimodal curricular transformation in their local contexts. Therein, I emphasized the effectiveness of feminist administrative practices, treating resistance to curricular transformation as a productive space in which directors and (resistant) teaching faculty might discuss and re-align pedagogical and curricular values, and utilizing professional development to create opportunities for all in the program to cultivate the expertise that is necessary to teach (multimodal) composition. Not least, Chapter 2 presented the finding that several programs utilized programmatic documents as a starting point for multimodal curricular transformation. Taking up this finding, Chapter 3 illustrated the ways in which one kind of document, specifically the outcomes statement, can make space for or preclude certain kinds of curricular content, like multimodal composing. I offered suggestions for how the language utilized within those documents might be adapted or revised to align with the version of composition articulated in our scholarship. This is vital work, I contend, in efforts toward multimodal curricular transformation, because of the ways in which documents construct and participate within the complex rhetorical ecologies of composition programs, articulating to internal and external audiences what it is we (purport to) care for in FYC. These documents cannot be overlooked or underestimated in processes of curricular transformation. Similarly, assignments deliver to students our curricular-programmatic visions. In other words, they animate our outcomes. To that end, this chapter seeks to answer the question, what does a transformed multimodal composition curriculum ask students to accomplish? To work toward an answer to the overall question, I utilize interview data and programmatic documents (outcomes, mission statements, etc.) to examine selected assignments within the case study curricula.

In planning the research project that would eventually become this book, I anticipated locating a wide range of multimodal assignment

https://doi.org/10.7330/9781646422135.c004

options from the case studies. This chapter, then, would have presented the limitations and affordances of various possibilities from which readers could select what seemed most appropriate and fitting for their respective programs. However, as was the case in Chapter 2, there was remarkable consistency across case studies: nine out of the ten programs require a version of what might be termed a remediation project.[1] In these projects, students (re)shape previously composed material (most often a research project/paper) for a different audience, utilizing a different medium, genre, or constellation of modes. In other words, these projects ask students to engage (multimodal) rhetoric. To present these findings, I will establish how remediation as a semiotic practice and the remediation project are detailed and theorized in scholarship before moving into how the case study programs detail such projects. I will illustrate that some of these projects are more aligned with the version of (multimodal) composition outlined in contemporary scholarship, asking students to exhibit a nuanced material-rhetorical flexibility through agentive choices. I will also highlight the other programmatic documents, like mission statements and outcomes, that these projects animate, revealing that, while including a multimodal assignment within the curriculum is a step toward multimodal curricular transformation, it is not the only step. To make progress toward multimodal curricular transformation, programs must work across documents and platforms to present a vision of composition that includes multimodal composition. Readers will thus leave this chapter with an understanding of how programmatic documents constellate into a culture that positions multimodality squarely within the content of composition.

SITUATING THE REMEDIATION PROJECT

Kathleen Blake Yancey (2004b) claims that "what we ask students to do is who we ask them to be" (p. 738). In other words, the assignments that we require students to complete as part of our composition curricula inevitably affect what and how they learn and what they might take with them when they leave our classrooms. Scholarship in multimodal composition and writing studies has argued clearly and persuasively that we should be preparing students to emerge from our programs "exhibiting a more nuanced awareness of the various choices they make throughout the process . . . and the effect those choices might have on

---

1. Program 6 decided not to share specific assignment descriptions with me, and there are no descriptions of that program's assignments publicly available online. This is why that program is left out of the analysis in this chapter.

others" (Shipka, 2013, p. 76), so that they might be able to engage in the "transfer, reformulation, and redesign of existing texts and meaning-making practices from one context to another" (Angay-Crowder et al., 2013, p. 38). This, as I have argued, is the *new* work of composition programs—using a wider semiotic repertoire of meaning-making to communicate with those beyond the academy (Bearden, 2019b), achieving and enacting what the New London Group terms *transformed practice*, which is the ability to make meaning across contexts and cultures (Cope & Kalantzis, 2000). To make critical interventions in our students' composing practices and to help them become effective composers in the twenty-first century, we must consider for whom they might compose beyond the academy, in the process reconsidering what our assignments ask them to do and subsequently who those assignments ask them to be.

Recently, teacher-scholars in writing studies have begun to explore the various multimodal assignments that we offer to students and the practices that those assignments value. Rory Lee (2018), for example, has outlined, among others, the following types of multimodal assignments:

> *First, social media is the most commonly analyzed and created multimodal text,* tied for number one for both practices across undergraduate major programs in Writing and Rhetoric. *Second, students often analyze and create blogs*: along with social media, they are the most commonly analyzed multimodal text, and they are the third most commonly created text, behind only social media and presentations. *Third,* although social media and blogs are analyzed and created most frequently, *students regularly analyze and create other multimodal texts too—for instance, brochures/pamphlets, flyers, web pages, and a specific type of web page: the digital portfolio.* (emphasis original)

Lee's list demonstrates two points: (a) when we do actually include multimodality within the composition curriculum (see Chapter 3 for a reminder of how frequently we do not), we (can) offer students a wide range of multimodal assignments, both digital and otherwise, simultaneously offering a range of the kinds of composers that they might be/become; and (b) this range suggests that it is perhaps less important that we require our students to compose a certain kind of text and more important that they gain practice crafting multiple kinds of texts, becoming flexible, adaptive communicators in the process. In doing so, students "develop composing strategies that can be used in multiple contexts" (Bearden, 2019b, p. 76), thereby achieving the overarching goal of a transformed multimodal composition curriculum *and* the vision of composition outlined in professional documents, like the WPA OS, which anticipates that "their [students'] abilities will diversify along disciplinary, professional, and civic lines as these writers move into new settings where expected outcomes expand, multiply, and diverge" (CWPA, 2014). New settings and new contexts require new (multimodal) ways of composing. Multimodal curricular transformation, I contend, is the way to ensure that all students who move through our programs are exposed to this vision of composition.

The remediation project is part of the way these case study programs enact this multiplicity, flexibility, and adaptability. While I derive the term "remediation" from Jay David Bolter and Richard Grusin's (1999) book of the same name, I am not quite operating from their definition. They define remediation as "the way in which one medium is seen by our culture as reforming or improving upon another" (p. 59), and "the formal logic by which new media refashion prior media forms" (p. 273). Thus, the term as originally conceived explores the relationships between media and how newer media repurpose their predecessors. For example, the term "scrolling" comes from manuscript culture before the time of the codex (literally, the scroll), but has been appropriated to describe moving up or down screens on computers or handheld devices. However, the definition of remediation has been expanded by those who study semiotics. Paul Prior and Julie Hengst (2010), for example, write that "semiotic remediation thus represents a *basic dialogic process* that interdiscursively *weaves together modes, media, genres, and events* and serves as a foundation for indexical and chronotopic orders" (p. 6, emphasis added). Elaborating on (and perhaps clarifying) Prior and Hengst's claim, Grabill and Blythe (2010) state that remediation describes the ways in which "content is recontextualized (repurposed) in new situations" (p. 185). This emphasis on the rhetorical (re)shaping of content has also been considered by Gunther Kress's (2010) work on multimodal communication. The terms that he utilizes, though, are translation and transduction. Translation, per Kress, is "a process in which meaning is moved. It is moved 'across,' 'transported'—from mode to mode; from one modal ensemble to another; from one mode in one culture to that 'same' mode in another culture" (p. 124), while transduction more specifically "names the process of moving meaning-material from one mode to another" (p. 125). This cluster of terms from media studies and semiotics emphasizes the multiple and varied meaning-making potentialities of different materials and the ways in which content *must* be rhetorically modified according to those potentialities. In synthesizing this work, we can perceive remediation as a literate practice, one that involves the (rhetorical) repurposing, recontextualizing, and revision of content for new contexts.

Operating from this definition, writing studies has examined remediation's position within composition curricula and the role of rhetoric in remediation. Kara Poe Alexander et al. (2016), for example, offer a definition of *adaptive* remediation and its role in the transfer of composing knowledge, writing that it is

> a set of strategies composers can draw on in order to adapt or reshape composing knowledge across media. Adaptive remediation assumes that a rhetorical choice that works well in one context or medium (e.g., a print-based essay) might not work as well in another (e.g., a digital story or other multimodal text). However, adaptive remediation also assumes that *composers can be trained to think about their motives or rhetorical purposes in ways that allow them to reshape and remediate their composing knowledge from one medium into another* (p. 34, emphasis added).

Remediation, as a part of the composition curriculum, highlights the different capacities of different modes, media, technologies, genres, and platforms and emphasizes the importance of being able to make informed composing choices within those capacities. Not least, Alexander et al.'s allusion to rhetoric suggests that rhetorical knowledge could help students perform more effectively within those differing contexts. As I have argued here and elsewhere (Bearden, 2019a), rhetoric offers a way for students to theorize the choices that they make in the composing process, making it an inextricable part of a transformed multimodal composition curriculum. In a discussion of the revisions made to their own composition program in the process of curricular transformation, Adsanatham et al. (2013) write, "As multimodal composing percolated through our program goals, it influenced rhetorical outcomes the most, not merely the composing skills, as might be first imagined" (p. 287). Similarly, Fordham and Oakes (2013) make the case for perceiving "rhetoric as the transmodal frame, the metalanguage, for our approach to multiliteracies . . . [which helps students] cultivate a more critical consciousness about communication in their everyday lives" (p. 318). This is because rhetoric includes "the ability to critically analyze a communication situation and to employ strategies and media that are appropriate to that situation. Rhetorical sensitivity inevitably must transcend specific skills in the use of discrete or even integrated modalities" (p. 331). Thus, having students engage in the process(es) and practice(s) of (semiotic) (adaptive) remediation makes them more capable and aware composers because, in acts of remediation, it is less important that students compose a specific kind of multimodal text and more important that they utilize rhetoric to theorize the process of text-making. To put it plainly, rhetoric provides a way to enact remediation, and remediation heightens students' understanding of rhetoric.

This symbiotic relationship between remediation and rhetoric has benefits for students. In *Toward a Composition Made Whole,* Jody Shipka (2011) argues that having students make choices in their composing processes is beneficial because of "the responsibility it places on students to determine the purposes of their work and how best to achieve them," which also "facilitates flexibility and metacommunicative awareness without predetermining for students the specific genres, media, and audiences with which they will work" (p. 87). In cultivating this meta-awareness, Crystal VanKooten (2016) argues that students gain the "ability to move consistently between enacting compositional choices and articulating how and why those choices are or might be effective or ineffective within a rhetorical context." Students can and do compose multimodally beyond the context of our curricula, but these composerly behaviors (making choices and being able to articulate the rationales of their choices) are increased with multimodal composing in the composition program. Ferruci and Derosa (2019) make the argument that "our students can both articulate and address complex audiences in ways that surpass their ability to do so when asked to write more traditional, alphabetic texts. *We have seen this tendency no matter what kind of text students write*" (pp. 220–221). Multimodal composition helps students understand better and differently the implications of their choices in the composing process—it also increases their understanding of composition overall. Asking our students to engage in such a practice allows us to make critical interventions into our students' composing practices and processes.

In the case study programs that are the focus of this chapter, remediation as a semiotic-rhetorical practice crystallizes into an assignment offered to students. In its descriptions, the assignment has gone by different names in different publications, but it asks students to take a previously-composed work, most typically a research paper, and then "remediate" it, per the definition offered in the above paragraphs. In the teaching for transfer (TFT) curriculum, this involves students writing in multiple genres, engaging with key terms like context, composition, and circulation in the third unit of the curriculum (Yancey et al., 2014, p. 57). The authors describe the assignment in the following way: "Unit 3: Using key concepts/terms about writing, students *draw upon what they discovered and wrote about in the research phase* (unit 2) for the development of a strategically planned composition in multiple genres, or 'Composition-in-three-genres'" (pp. 57–58, emphasis added). Thus, this project emphasizes three things: (a) student choice in the genres that they select based on their topics, audiences, purposes, and interests;

(b) rhetorical knowledge, which students demonstrate in a rationale delivered alongside the multi-text project; and (c) reflection, a text submitted by the students detailing what they learned about composing by engaging in the process (p. 75). Indeed, this combination is one of the most important features of the TFT curriculum:

> The composition-in-three genres project is a turning point for many students in understanding the key terms for the course and beginning to appreciate the ways their knowledge about writing is situated in context. For this composition-in-three-genres assignment, *students draw on the second assignment, focused on their topics of individual interest, which is then repurposed for the new genres. Put simply, they work with this material in a new way.* Students appreciate that they can use the information they've just researched; they won't be distracted by searching for new material while designing a strategy for presenting this researched information to a real-world audience in a coherent composition.
>
> The purpose of the third assignment is also to help students *enact* key terms, and the rhetorical choices—which genres will work for which audience, for example, and what the purpose of the writing might be—help solidify the key terms and the ways they can be used to help conceptualize a writing task. (p. 142, emphasis added)

This is the work of the remediation project: working with existing material, providing students a way to cultivate material-rhetorical flexibility and rhetorical dexterity, choosing materials that are most appropriate for their purposes and audiences rather than focusing on the generation of new content or arguments, etc. In following this model, students theorize and utilize a robust model of composing, making, and sharing meaning and knowledge with multiple kinds of materials shaped for audiences including but not limited to the academy.

In the review of scholarship provided here, it should go without saying that this work is not easy; multimodal composition via remediation is not an easier or less rigorous alternative to alphabetic writing or other kinds of multimodal composing. Carrie Leverenz (2014) speaks to the difficulty here, arguing that we

> must accept our limited control over the materials we work with and the contingent nature of the effects we wish to produce, even as we must continue to engage with those materials in an attempt to produce an effect. The fact that students need to learn to use writing effectively in spite of their limited control over writing is one reason the teaching of writing is also irresolvably complex. The position of composition within universities adds to its wickedness: it is a course we are required to teach and that students are required to take because it is assumed we can prepare them to write well in other courses, even though there is little evidence that such a goal is achievable. (p. 4)

Several others speak to the complexity of learning to compose multi-modally as well (VanKooten & Berkley, 2016; Wardle, 2012; Purdy, 2014), and while I know at this point in the book that I do not need to argue for the value of multimodal composition or outline its (possible) position within the composition curriculum, it is important to note a distinction here. Whereas some of the research that I have invoked earlier in this book focuses on multimodal composition as a literate practice taking place outside of the academy, these voices focus specifically on how multimodality manifests *within assignments delivered to students.* These kinds of assignments do not "dumb down" the composing process for students or challenge the rigor of the composition curriculum: they heighten students' (meta)awareness of their composing choices. They enrich students' composing processes. They return to and remind us of the importance of rhetoric as the full available means of persuasion, not just composing alphabetic text for academic audiences.

What readers will find most promising in this chapter is that, while the assignments offered in these case study programs are less complicated—they do not require that students create ensembles of texts, like the TFT curriculum does, or ask students to complete so many pages of reflection and rhetorical rationale—they do still ask students to engage in the process of remediation, taking an assignment (typically a traditional research paper) and recontextualizing it for a new purpose, audience, genre, etc. In other words, programs can invoke the messiness and complexity of remediation without crafting an assignment as multi-faceted as the one detailed in the TFT curriculum. I should note here, however, that remediation is not the only way to bring about multimodal curricular transformation. Like Lee describes above, there are many ways to incorporate multimodal composition at the programmatic level that do not involve students starting with precomposed material and then modifying that for a different context, audience, or purpose. As just one example, in *Toward a Composition Made Whole* (2011), Jody Shipka describes a classroom history assignment that asks students to represent, using materials of their own choosing, the events of a particular class. A research paper or alphabetic essay is not a required "first step" in that process. Another alternative would involve students starting with the mul-timodal and then moving to the alphabetic in the remediation process. We do not always have to begin with—and defer to—the primacy of print.

However, as I mentioned at the beginning of this chapter, nine out of the ten case study programs described this kind of remediation as the way in which multimodal curricular transformation manifested within their programs. This consistency suggests that the inclusion of a remediation project is perhaps the project of least resistance because of the way in which it includes and utilizes print, alphabetic writing as part of the multimodal composing process. In the remainder of this chapter, I will trace various incarnations of the remediation project present within the case studies. There is, I argue, a spectrum of options—certain programs require that all students complete the same kind of remediation, while others allow instructors and students to make their own choices in the process. The latter end of the spectrum more closely aligns with the vision of a multimodal composition curriculum currently detailed in scholarship. Regardless of their position on the spectrum, though, remediation projects can help programs initiate multimodal curricular transformation because they emphasize and require rhetorical knowledge and material flexibility—the foundations of a transformed multimodal composition curriculum.

ITERATIONS OF REMEDIATION

To reiterate, nine of the ten case studies included at least one remediation, and two included more than one. However, not all programs included the same kind of remediation project: some programs require that all students in the program compose the same kind of remediated text (e.g., a digital portfolio or a digital editorial) while others allow students to choose the final form of their projects. Like the findings that I presented in Chapter 3 on outcomes, the assignments that are the most effective in this regard *do not prescribe the materials with/in which students work.* Allowing the students this choice provides them with rhetorical agency and responsibility, thereby deepening their understanding of materials/materialities, semiotic resources, rhetoric, and subsequently their own composing processes. As important, these projects are supported by other programmatic documents that accumulate into a culture that values and necessitates multimodal composition. Remediation, in other words, has the potential to work toward multimodal curricular transformation, but simply adding a multimodal project to a composition curriculum does not equal transformation. This work requires a consistent commitment to multimodality across texts.

First, two of the case study programs require that students perform a *specific kind of remediation predetermined by the program.* This approach has limitations and affordances: these programs ensure a consistent multimodal experience by having students create the same kind of text, but this does not allow students to make their own choices about the forms, genres, and media in which they work. Instead of emphasizing choice or material-rhetorical flexibility, this approach focuses on the process of rhetorically reshaping content. I would argue that these programs bridge the gap between minimally multimodal programs that have not yet entered into multimodal curricular transformation (e.g., those that offer a low-stakes multimodal assignment at the end of the semester or make it a choice for individual instructors) and those that simply assign students with a task and allow the students to determine the final form/ format of their projects based on their individual rhetorical goals. In other words, individuals that are interested in working toward multi-modal curricular transformation but are concerned with projects vary-ing widely (for assessment purposes or because of instructor discomfort) might look to these programs as an example. Program 2, for example, requires that all students in the program compose a final digital port-folio using Wordpress. I argue that portfolio assemblage constitutes an act of remediation because, in assembling a portfolio, students engage in acts of collection, selection, and reflection (Yancey, 1998; Yancey, 2001), all of which are acts of *rhetorical reshaping*. In the introduction to *A Rhetoric of Reflection*, Yancey writes (2016),

> Through the practice of reflection, we draw on what is culturally known and infuse, interweave, integrate it with what we as individuals know—cognitively, affectively, and socially—to make a new knowledge that draws from the extant but is not a replication of it, that is, instead, unique, a knowledge only each one of us can make as it is in dialogue with what is. Not least, that new knowledge, collectively enacted, changes the very cultures situating reflective practice. (p. 11)

Reflection, then, and the intertextual connections tying a portfolio to-gether, are deeply rhetorical. In creating a portfolio, students increase their rhetorical flexibility by abstracting what they learn in one context and thinking through how that might transfer to another. *Digital* port-folios, like those required by Program 2, constitute even more complex acts of rhetorical work because they ask "students to write for the screen as well as for the page; to create relationships between and among linked material, as between and among experiences; to update [them] as a hab-it of mind; and to represent learning in part by exploring the connec-tions the digital environment invites" (Yancey, 2004b, p. 754). They are a different kind of composing, one that more accurately reflects the cur-rent communicative landscape: in highlighting the concept of audience, in anticipating circulation, in making it possible for students to return to and revise their portfolios (and how they present themselves), digi-tal portfolios constitute a necessarily multimodal translation of content for different audiences, purposes, etc. As such, they invite the kind of learning that multimodal theory values. Indeed, the director of Program 2 stated, "I really wanted it [the required portfolio] to be digital, because of the way it *enlivens the rhetorical canon.*" This programmatic attention to multimodal rhetoric manifests across documents, too. The program's website includes a page that describes the digital portfolio, emphasizing that design is an important part of the assignment, particularly in terms of how the consistency, color, and contrast impact the readability of the portfolio for its audience. Additionally, two of the program's outcomes ask students to consider rhetorical terms in writing situations and to "understand and use" multiple technologies to "address a range of audiences." While this program requires the same digital portfolio of all students, thereby prescribing the kind of remediation that students perform, the assignment description *in conjunction with other programmatic documents* highlights rhetorical considerations and (re)shaping material in terms of audience, which are part of the goals of a transformed multimodal composition curriculum.

Similarly, in Program 7, students compose a digital editorial that asks them to (re)present the research that they conducted for a previous assignment in an online space. The editorial fosters in students the ability to compose for nonacademic, public audiences through the combination of image, text, and web platform. The director described this activity as "one that we devised in order to really get students to pay attention to hyperlinks, the multimodal aspects of a digital piece, to notice ads and everything" as a way to cultivate "web literacy." Here the director emphasizes the importance of understanding the rhetorical situation and audience of the digital editorial as a way to cultivate a sense of how multimodal elements constellate on the Web. The program scaffolds the project in such a way that all students *must* endeavor to understand which multimodal elements would be effective for their chosen publication's rhetorical situation. Specifically, the students do a genre analysis of the publication to which they would like to submit the editorial and a medium analysis of the formal features of the publication itself. All of this increases students' attention to rhetoric and therefore prepares them to produce a multimodal text that "requires a lot of different kinds of literacies to understand it . . . what we tell them is when you're writing a lit review or something, that's a more top-down piece of writing. The writer gets to control the journey more or less," according to the director of Program 7. In the digital editorial, however, students work with

the hyperlink notion of literacy and when to open those, when to hyperlink some, how often and how frequently do you use them? There's the framing, the colors, the visuals, the images, the picture of the writer, the bio is a whole separate kind of thing, the ads surrounding it, ancillary links to related articles. I mean, there's a lot that goes on and then there's the things like the fonts and bolding and so forth and where and how it's positioned on a page, etc. A lot of different things that you have to read and control as a *rhetorician*. (emphasis added)

This makes it clear that, while students are working with/in a digital space, they are not merely learning how to work the technology. Rather, they are thinking through the rhetorical implications of their composerly choices, especially how multiple modes constellate on the digital page to make meaning for the audience.

In cultivating this web sensibility, the director was careful to emphasize that the project and the way in which the project is scaffolded is (still) intellectually rigorous:

We make them [students] suffer the agonies of academics. They develop an academic specialty. Then we make them pitch a fake pitch basically: "I'm an expert in human cognition." La la la. Whatever it happens to be, "and I want to do this piece." One of my favorites from this year was a student of mine who did human cognition. She did it on color and on color perception. Then she went from there to the editorial. I think it was Marie Claire, and it was about what colors to wear for a job interview. So, she positioned herself as an expert in color perception. They [the students] are really thinking about audience in all sorts of interesting ways, and her piece was colorful. She had pictures of women in yellow, because yellow is the color to wear, a little bit of yellow, just so you know. She got to learn about something that she *got to actually use in a way*. (emphasis added)

And in our conversation, the director argued that there are multiple rhetorical benefits to this theory-practice rhetorical approach to multimodal composition:

There are students who can do academic writing just fine, but now we're thinking of them as people who lift weights or something. They're so used to doing one set of things, they can't move. So, they can't do it [write for a non-academic audience]. Then meanwhile some of the students who are not very good at academic writing really do take to this. They take to it visually. They show their visual-rhetorical skills. They're so smart with how they work with the images . . . those are more often than not what we would conventionally call the not very good writers who suddenly are shining at the end with their creativity and adapting their lit reviews and with creating the site [that houses the digital editorial].

Through this description, it is clear that the project fosters what Graban et al. (2013) call rhetorical dexterity, and what I have called material-rhetorical flexibility (Bearden, 2019b). It is less important here that students write for a specific audience or purpose outside of the academy and more important that they simply get practice composing with different materials than those to which they have become accustomed, understanding what those different materials allow them to say or do. I find the language this director utilized regarding weightlifting particularly helpful. So often, our students enter our classrooms with various degrees of experience or success in the mode of alphabetic writing. They might possess strength in that kind of writing, but scholarship informs us that flexibility and dexterity in multiple modes are more useful skills that will serve students more in future contexts. This particular project helps students work toward that by emphasizing the rhetorical shaping of researched material for a specific publication, audience, and/or genre *and* requiring that they compose multimodally by utilizing visuals, including links, and making layout/design choices. Projects like these, even those that require students to work with predetermined materials, emphasize the composerly dexterity/flexibility that we want students to cultivate by the end of FYC. These projects, as one way to work toward multimodal curricular transformation, enliven what we have always claimed to value, synthesizing complex rhetorical actions and considerations within the composition curriculum through remediation in a way that might be more accessible for programs concerned about consistent programmatic assessment or instructor resistance/technological inexperience.

On the other end of the continuum, six of the case study programs did not prescribe the texts that students create or the means by which they create them. As I have argued in this book, programs remain vital by adapting with student needs, disciplinary advances, and local changes. An assignment that works well for students in the current moment might not work well in the future. Requiring specific technologies or texts has the potential to freeze a program within a specific moment in time. The director of Program 5 referenced this potential as we discussed fluctuations in multimodal assignments over time:

> There were, early on, three different versions of an audio PSA. You know, different audiences or different arguments. We had a whole lot of those. We got bored of them. Prezi had its moment. Blogging and Weebly and Wix have had their moments. Video, which is something that I am really interested in, definitely had its moment along the way. Increasingly what I'm seeing is less of one thing. . . . Instead students choose something of their own model. I've seen hand-drawn graphic novels—well not full graphic novels—but short graphics. Or performance poetry. I think if anything that [choosing a specific kind of multimodal text for students to complete] moved us toward the open model, because *we got tired of some of the genres that started to sediment.* (emphasis added)

This director makes the point that the materials with which students compose are not as important as the act of rhetorical transformation via remediation. By allowing students to make their own choices in the final format and circulation of their texts, the remediation project can make space for emerging technologies and literacies that students might bring to the classroom, keeping the curriculum responsive *and* in line with the goals of multimodal curricular transformation, which include cultivating a rhetorical metalanguage and awareness, material-rhetorical flexibility/dexterity, and the ability to compose in/for multiple contexts and rhetorical situations.

And to be clear, these more flexible projects require that students choose *effective* means of making and sharing meaning, not simply those that are easily or most visibly multimodal. A few of the directors that I interviewed used PowerPoint as an example of an unacceptable vehicle for remediation because the platform, while clearly multimodal, can be rhetorically ineffective in practice. The director at Program 10 mentioned, "That's what the students just default to, and they just take big chunks of their research paper and plunk it into PowerPoint and think it's multimodal enough." For this director, the issue was not with PowerPoint as a tool of remediation, but with the ways in which students uncritically defer to that platform and its rhetorical constraints. Similarly, in Program 9, the director stated that students cannot "just choose a PowerPoint, because you're making a bullshit decision. You're going to make a PowerPoint because it *serves very specific rhetorical goals.*" Indeed, in these programs it is important that students make critical, intentional choices in terms of the materials that they utilize to create effective remediations. The director at Program 9 described the remediation project there in the following way:

> The students just have to write *to an audience,* and if they're gonna choose an academic one, then they better have a pretty good reason for choosing an academic audience, and they better know the genres and what it is that they're deciding to do. So, rather than just thinking about academic conversations, *they really start the process at a different point,* which says, now that you've done all of this research on X—four or five weeks of research. . . . So, now once they're there—who do you want to talk to? This is how we bring *rhetoric forward. Who is your audience? What's your genre? What's your medium?* (emphasis added)

Students must make choices informed by their knowledge of rhetoric and not based on what they believe will be easiest. In other words, flexibility does not make the project any less rigorous.

For these programs, the remediation project is preceded by a more traditional alphabetic research project. Program 10's director provided an overview of the task, stating, "It's a *repurposing of the research paper,* which is usually, I'm guessing, six to ten pages. The students do a multimodal repurposing of that in which they have to do the statement of goals and purposes kind of thing and audience analysis. All of that. Then, they present that to the class and rethink the research and how it could be delivered in a different way" (emphasis added). Starting with the content originally developed in the research paper gives students the opportunity to focus on the rhetorical reshaping of material. The "statement of goals and purposes" the director references here is similar to what Jody Shipka has described as a goals and choices statement, which students compose alongside their multimodal texts. These statements allow students to articulate and rationalize the rhetorical decisions they make as they complete tasks. The benefit of having students do both—remediate their work for a new context *and* detail how and why that remediation came into being—includes students' understanding that the "materiality and the delivery, reception, and circulation of texts, objects, and events are no longer viewed as separate . . . but as integral parts of invention and production processes" (2005, p. 301). By engaging in this kind of work, the program achieves two of its outcomes, which include responding appropriately to "different rhetorical situations" and utilizing the "available and appropriate composing modalities" to do so, revealing the connection between programmatic values (plurality, flexibility, etc.) and the assignments that instantiate those values.

Program 1 offers a similar kind of project to the one described by Program 10's director. Resources made available to instructors on the program's website label the project as a "creative remediation" of the research paper. The director at Program 1 described the task associated with this project as "presenting this work you [students] have done to a broader audience than this boring research paper you've written to this class." By speaking to this broader audience, students engage one of the program's outcomes, which asks them to utilize rhetorical knowledge by "using the means of persuasion appropriate" to the context, listing off writing, images, and sounds as possible means for doing so. Indeed, the program's website defines "other semiotic codes such as sound and images" as part of the content of the program's curriculum. These multimodal-rhetorical values articulated by the director, by the program's outcomes, and by the program's public-facing website crystallize in the remediation project, which delivers those values to students. Indeed, the constellation of these documents and the values they articulate, enact, and embody *is* multimodal curricular transformation. The remediation project is but one piece of a larger genre ecology.

That ecology extends university-wide at Program 4, where the remediation project manifests as texts intended to be shared at a semi-annual event that celebrates student writing. The director there describes this event as a kind of science fair for writing, wherein students "move from the more conventionally-approached, research-based, academic writing project to something that circulates differently in terms of reaching out and making itself accessible to a public." In short, the students take a research project that they have composed earlier in the semester and transform it into a public, interactive multimodal text that they share at the celebration. One of the programs' outcomes reads that students can be expected to demonstrate the ability to adapt their "writing to distinct rhetorical contexts," with particular consideration for "the way composition *transforms* across contexts and forms." The presentation and circulation of their research at the celebration requires that students utilize a wider material-rhetorical repertoire because academic writing would not be effective within that context. Other outcomes for this program require that students "consciously construct persuasive texts" and identify "rhetorical qualities" within composing situations. Thus, like Program 1, Program 4 presents multiple programmatic documents that detail the importance of multimodal composition. In so doing, these remediation projects and the programmatic-textual ecologies in which they participate emphasize and synthesize the key terms and concepts we associate with FYC and articulate in our professional documents, like the WPA OS: audience, purpose, genre, context, etc. In other words, they have the potential to align the content of our curricula more closely with disciplinary advances and have the potential to move us in the direction of multimodal curricular transformation, and while remediation projects are not the only way to do this, the data here suggests that they are at least one productive possibility.

Program 5 provides an even stronger example of the capacity of remediation projects to enact our disciplinary values at the curricular level and work toward multimodal curricular transformation. According to a website detailing the curriculum at Program 5, remediation projects constitute an opportunity for students to develop an understanding regarding how "the medium affects the message" by remediating a prior researched writing project in order to deliver their "work to a new audience." Such a project synthesizes at least three of the program's outcomes:

- One related to multimodal-rhetorical performance, which expects students to demonstrate an awareness of the "unique limitations and affordances" of different communicative "technologies and modalities";

- one related to more general rhetorical knowledge, which expects students to compose "effectively for different contexts, audiences, purposes, and genres"; and
- one pertaining to reflection that asks students to consider their rhetorical decisions, especially as they pertain to the technologies of "production and reception" of their work.

In fact, in the interview that I conducted with the director of Program 5, he argued that the structure of the program's curriculum *leads to and culminates in* the remediation project, revealing how integral that project is to the overall program. In describing the scaffolding of the course, he said:

> We begin with some kind of short initial reflective writing about experiences with writing and rhetoric and beliefs about writing and rhetoric coming into the course. We do a rhetorical analysis assignment then move into a researched public argument assignment. . . . Then the next assignment in the sequence is our remediation assignment where students return to one of the first three assignments and transform the argument for that assignment into a different medium and genre for a different audience. It's very open and flexible.

There are three points that I would like to emphasize here. First, the program does not prescribe the final form of the remediation or the specific kind of multimodal composition that students perform—it only requires that students work with materials that expand textual possibilities beyond the purview of academic, alphabetic writing and audiences. This allows students to make their own choices, cultivating rhetorical agency and responsibility *in addition to* working toward the program's goals, values, and outcomes in the process. Second, alongside the required remediation is "a really substantial reflective component. That's actually required for each one of our essays—it's accompanied by some sort of reflective writing about rhetorical choices and learning, but we encourage an even deeper and longer reflection on the remediation." These reflective pieces often accompany remediation projects, offering students the ability to articulate and defend the choices they make in the act of transformation, which increases their understanding of (multimodal) rhetoric. This reminds us that alphabetic writing is not done away with in programs that center multimodal composition; it is simply repositioned within a larger constellation of semiotic possibilities available to students. Third, this assignment is the *culmination* of the curriculum. It is not an ancillary add-on to the end of the semester. Rather, the remediation project instantiates and animates many of the program's outcomes simultaneously, demonstrating what I would suggest is the most robust and nuanced example of a *single* remediation project situated within the transformed composition curricula of these case studies. According to the director of Program 5,

> We did a full portfolio assessment as part of this process [of entering into multimodal curricular transformation], and one of the things that we found was that the *remediation project seemed to be the place where students were demonstrating the most reflective metacognition and the most rhetorical knowledge especially when it came to audience awareness*. Compared to some of the other angles, we were able to demonstrate it wasn't just meeting the digital-multimodal rhetoric outcome. The act of composing to an audience they cared about in a *medium and genre* they cared about actually seemed to lead to better audience awareness and reflection on the audience. (emphasis added)

To put it plainly, the infusion of multimodal composition into this program's curriculum took place through the requirement of its remediation project but also through its outcomes, public website, and other programmatic documents. At the intersection of those documents, the program delivers to students a unified and transformed vision of composition, one that, according to the programmatic assessment the director here references, increases their knowledge of audience, their understanding of the communicative potentialities of different resources, and their ability to cross contexts, reaching new audiences through multimodal means. Assignments like the remediation project are part of multimodal curricular transformation, but transformation requires a multitextual programmatic approach.

Two of the case study programs enact this on a larger scale by including multiple multimodal projects within their curricula, thereby exhibiting what I would argue is a more thorough commitment to multimodal composition curricula and transformation. Program 8 requires two different kinds of remediations in its course sequence as a way of delivering what it terms a "newly revised, multi-modal curriculum," which involves teaching students to "compose in a variety of genres and media." In so doing, the program seeks to prepare students for academic and professional contexts in addition to "their civic responsibilities . . . and lives." The remediations include a culminating digital portfolio that requires that students attend to the (multimodal) elements of web design and a documentary film or advocacy website (students pick one or the other) that presents research conducted over the course of the semester and presented in previous assignments. Like Program 7, Program 8 scaffolds the remediation project for students by having them complete inquiry proposals and genre analyses to collect the research that the remediation will share and consider the most effective means and modes for presenting that research. To reiterate, allowing students to utilize the same base content—in this context, previously conducted research—to create their remediation allows students to focus on the multimodal-rhetorical aspects of the project: how design choices, image foci, color contrast, etc. impact their chosen audiences and inflect their composerly goals.

Program 3 requires multiple multimodal assignments and makes references to the importance of multimodal composition across programmatic documents: outcomes, program website, and assignments. The program's public website presents a definition of composition that includes "multiple modes of expression," detailing that "design and analyzing visual and multimodal texts" will be part of the expected work of the program. This articulation communicates to students, instructors, and other stakeholders that multimodality is a meaningful, inextricable part of the composition curriculum, which includes a research proposal/annotated bibliography, a researched argument (in other words, an alphabetic research paper), a remediation, and a multimodal argument. Within the remediation project, students create what the program calls "visual arguments." In describing this assignment, the director stated that students "*translate* their research paper, mounting their own argument and using visuals" (emphasis added). The guidelines for the project are fairly simple: "It has to be an argument. That's the goal. It has to represent the same amount of effort, composition, design, and rhetorical considerations of audience [as the research paper], and they do a reflective piece afterwards." To summarize, in the visual argument, students create a rhetorically effective text *remediated from* a previous assignment, utilizing their rhetorical knowledge of visuals to compose a multimodal text. While the project utilizes and builds off of content developed within a previous project, massaging that content into a different form/format/medium for a potentially different audience is a complex compositional task. It is, to echo DePalma (2015), a nuanced act of "rhetorical reshaping . . . in which composers remix, repurpose, recontextualize, or coordinate semiotic resources across tasks, media, and contexts in order to fulfill their rhetorical objectives" (p. 627). This coordination of resources expands the version of "composition" delivered to students by asking them to compose with more than just alphabetic writing using rhetorical considerations to do so.

Such an assignment highlights the necessity of rhetorical knowledge, requires students to engage in remediation, and therefore instantiates and animates multimodal curricular transformation, providing one possible multimodal assignment for instructors and administrators to consider making a meaningful part of their composition curricula. I would be remiss, however, if I did not note the limitations of this particular assignment. By prescribing the visual, the project is inherently ableist. As I mentioned in the previous chapter, such assignments elide the fact that people with visual impairments exist and (are required to) take composition courses. Additionally, in her description of the visual argument project, this director implied that the argument preceded *and superseded* the visuals or that the visual cannot be a source of invention. Alphabetic, print literacy is still the primary mode of thinking in this example. While we can offer a range of multimodal assignments to students, and while those multimodal assignments can do good work for certain students, we must be mindful of the kinds of multimodal assignments we create in our efforts toward curricular transformation, especially in terms of the "hospitality" (to invoke the language of Yergeau et al.) of those assignments. This particular example is a step in the right direction but could be revised even further. For example, it could be as simple as "make your argument in a different medium than alphabetic writing, taking into consideration the ways in which different media have different constraints and possibilities."

The program also includes another multimodal project that is not a remediation. This project has the same "argument" requirement as the visual remediation, but this assignment is less prescriptive, simply requiring that students present the history of something related to campus life. In the assignment description available on the program's website, collages, videos, websites, and many other kinds of multimodal (both digital and not) texts are listed as possibilities for the final form that student projects can take. It is more important here that students consider the design and meaning-making potentialities of the kind of text that they want to create and how that will impact/influence the argument that they want to make. This enacts the capacious version of rhetoric I discussed in Chapter 3 that makes space for multimodal composing. Indeed, this program includes an outcome from WPA OS 2.0: "Understand and exploit the differences in the rhetorical strategies and in the affordances available for both print and electronic composing processes and texts." This is not an act of remediation as this chapter has defined it: students do not come to the project with material composed for another context. Rather, they are considering and engaging the different rhetorical affordances of whatever medium they think will be the most effective for conveying their argument at the same time as they are inventing and arranging that argument. This, too, is the work of multimodal curricular transformation: a capacious rhetoric that gives students the opportunity to explore semiotic potentials. Should programs want to include multimodal composition within their curricula without including a remediation project, they might look to this as one example. It does, however, follow the same format as the other projects and programs detailed in this chapter: it is an instantiation and animation of larger programmatic goals and values articulated across programmatic documents, revealing and reinforcing the fact that multimodal curricular transformation is an ongoing, intentional, multitextual effort to infuse multimodality within composition curriculum by emphasizing rhetoric as the *full, available means of persuasion.*

SOME CONCLUSIONS

Reading across the multimodal projects that are integral parts of the composition curricula in these case study programs, we can distill a few useful insights that will be useful to readers who are interested in striving toward multimodal curricular transformation in their own contexts. The first insight is the overwhelming presence of the remediation project within the case studies. Nine out of ten case studies included remediation projects. The popularity of this project and the consistent form in which it appears—students taking research conducted for a prior, alphabetic assignment and rhetorically adapting it for a different audience—suggest that remediation is one way to bridge the gap between FYC's long history with alphabetic writing *and* contemporary trends in scholarship that advocate for multimodal composition. In the scaffolded approach detailed by these programs, students work with material with which they are already comfortable and familiar, and consequently, the task shifts, becoming an exercise in rhetorical knowledge and audience awareness. In the multimodal curricular transformations presented by these programs, alphabetic, researched writing remains but is positioned within a larger constellation of semiotic possibilities. Remediation, it seems, is a way to center rhetoric, to value multimodal possibilities, and to preserve our commitment to writing. Indeed, this could explain its popularity in the case study programs: It creates space within programmatic curricula for academic, alphabetic, researched writing, which has been one of the defining features of FYC, *and* multimodal composition, making space for our history while anticipating the future.

Second, these programs make the case that multimodal assignments like the remediation project instantiate and animate the values articulated in other programmatic documents. Most of the (remediation) projects that I detail in this chapter animate several programmatic goals and outcomes simultaneously, most of which are focused on audience awareness, material flexibility, and rhetorical performance. They enact programmatic visions and definitions of composition presented on public websites, mission statements, template syllabi, and elsewhere. Multimodal curricular transformation is a *cultural* shift for programs, and these case studies suggest that new culture accumulates from program documents and practices. Revising outcomes statements is not enough; including professional development opportunities is not enough; requiring a multimodal project is not enough. Multimodal curricular transformation requires all three to achieve the significant cultural shift necessary.

Third, these case studies reveal that there is no single project that will successfully bring about multimodal curricular transformation. In this chapter, I presented variations of the remediation project: Some of these programs require all students to complete the same kind of project (a digital editorial or a portfolio, for instance); in others, students are allowed to make their own choices in terms of medium, genre, and mode. This continuum, I argue, is useful for those who would like to attempt multimodal curricular transformation in their own programs but are concerned about instructor resistance or anxiety. As I mentioned in Chapter 2, instructors are likely to resist multimodal composition if they feel it challenges their authority/expertise—if all instructors are teaching toward the same kind of multimodal text, there is a built-in community of support upon which they might draw. Too, requiring the same assignment of all students in the program makes assessment of multimodal values and outcomes easier. However, this chapter demonstrates that some multimodal assignments are more useful than others: the projects that provide students with choice and require substantial reflection invite students to engage rhetoric, using a wider range of the available means of persuasion than alphabetic writing to achieve their purposes and goals in the way that contemporary scholarship contends that they should. In taking and repurposing previously composed research, students navigate a complex stream of semiotic resources, employing a theory of practice that attends to rhetoric, genre awareness, audience awareness, media/material flexibility, and goal-setting in the process. Programs will want to consider where they want to fall on this continuum in the short and long term in accordance with their values and goals.

Not least, I would be remiss if I did not highlight the fact that remediation is not the only project that can animate and instantiate multimodal curricular transformation—it was simply the most popular assignment in the case studies I examined for the purposes of this book. There are other ways to engage the audience awareness, material flexibility, and rhetorical knowledge that are part of multimodal curricular transformation. While these projects ask students to begin with a research-based, alphabetic text and then translate that into something multimodal, I can also imagine an altogether different task of presenting research multimodally *first.* Arguments—even academic arguments—can be made outside of print, and research can and should be shared in ways that circulate easily beyond the academy. This could be an assignment on its own, or as part of a sequence. Students might begin with the multimodal and then move into the alphabetic, reflecting on how the experiences are different and what they have learned about composing from that process. The sequencing of the remediation projects, as they are currently articulated by these programs, suggests that print, alphabetic writing is still primary. However, as Palmeri has argued, and as I have suggested in Chapter 3, we are still in the early stages of multimodal curricular transformation at the national level. These projects, while they do have limitations, do meaningfully integrate multimodality within composition curricula. As such, we might think of them as the first steps toward a new version of composition, one that sets students tasks, a la Shipka, without prescribing the materials with which they work. In that different FYC, students can practice composing with unfamiliar or familiar materials for various audiences, depending on their goals. Multimodal curricular transformation, thankfully, is not a singular event. It is a programmatic way of being, an intentional, ongoing, collaborative effort to deliver to students a vision of composition that embraces the full available means of persuasion. I expect that these programs might change the ways in which multimodality manifests in their programs in the future if they have not already done so in the time between data collection and the writing of this book. This is the complexity of multimodal curricular transformation: it is crafting assignments that value multimodal rhetorical practices, *and* it is achieving programmatic buy-in from the instructional staff responsible for delivering curriculum to students, *and* it is transforming the language in/around the documents that make up the program. In the next and final chapter of this book, I will synthesize my findings thus far, offering a heuristic for those who want to begin the process of multimodal curricular transformation in their own contexts. My hope is that readers will leave this book with a plan of action, a set of strategies to utilize for helping align their programs with the current state of writing studies.

5

AN EVOLVING HEURISTIC FOR MULTIMODAL CURRICULAR TRANSFORMATION

To be honest, this project and this book emerged out of frustration. At professional conferences, I have presented on multimodal meaning-making in medieval manuscripts, multimodal reading practices, and the role of rhetoric in a multimodal composition curriculum. However, the most frequent questions that I receive after my presentations are:

- What is multimodality?
- Can you give us an example of a multimodal assignment?

I found these questions disappointing the first few times that I received them, wondering if anyone was actually engaging with the arguments I was making. Over time, though, and through conversation, I came to understand that the attendees asking these questions were most often doing the work of administration with little support from their institutions. They came to learn introductory information about a concept that might help them bring innovation to their programs while I was operating from the naive assumption that everyone already knew what multimodality meant and what it looked like in programmatic practice. My faulty assumption is not unique. In response to an article I wrote describing how the program in which I work came to include multimodal composition and why other programs ought to do the same, a reviewer wrote something to the effect of "Everybody already does multimodality, so I don't see the point of this article." That reviewer, while perhaps ungenerous, was not necessarily wrong. Multimodality is indeed a central facet of communication and meaning-making, and to those who read widely in the scholarship of writing studies, it would be easy to assume that all instructors and administrators see its value and position within composition curricula. But this is simply not the case. As I argued in the first chapter of this book, there persists a disconnect between contemporary scholarship and the day-to-day work of composition programs, which remain overwhelmingly focused on print alphabetic writing, and

https://doi.org/10.7330/9781646422135.c005

models that explore how to revise entire programs to shift toward multimodal composition are in short supply.

Reflecting on these personal anecdotes and this disciplinary disconnect led me to the central question that this book has attempted to address: By what processes and practices can multimodal curricular transformation be realized? My goal has been to uncover ways we might systematically, meaningfully, and sustainably integrate multimodality within composition curricula by reading across programs and contexts to uncover transformative insights that can be extrapolated to different kinds of composition programs. While the nuances of curricular revision are contextually contingent, locally inflected, and idiosyncratic to the social interactions of the director and the teaching faculty who work together to deliver the curriculum, my research has led to an evolving set of considerations, a flexible heuristic, that might be taken up by those who are interested in bringing transformation to their institutions. In this final chapter, I will reiterate the arguments that this book has made and pose those arguments as a series of questions that can be utilized by programs to guide the process of multimodal curricular transformation.

Chapter 2 presented data collected from interviews with program directors who had initiated and/or participated in multimodal curricular transformation in their local contexts. The interviews yielded the following findings:

- Multimodal curricular transformation is motivated not by an interest in making use of the newest or flashiest technologies but rather by an awareness of the current communicative landscape and a desire to allow students to utilize the *full available means of persuasion*. The directors that I interviewed acknowledge the limitations of print, alphabetic writing, articulating that multimodal composition allows students the opportunity to increase their rhetorical potential.

- In the process(es) of multimodal curricular transformation, the directors utilized feminist pragmatic rhetorical strategies as a way to productively make use of resistance. Curricular revisions will always be met with resistance from certain individuals. However, these directors utilized moments of resistance as a moment of opportunity to have open, honest, reflective conversations about curricular values, moments in which it is possible for resistance instructors to find space within or connection to multimodal composition. Feminist administrative models like these work toward more equitable programs by including and honoring the voices of the teaching faculty working therein as they simultaneously make multimodal composition more accessible and less anxiety-inducing to those same faculty. Perhaps more important, these practices are *effective*—the directors that I interviewed were clear that transformation would not have been possible without the investment solicited by these administrative practices.

- Instructors tend to resist multimodal curricular transformation if they perceive the programmatic challenges as a threat to their teacherly ethos, authority, or expertise. Conversations about values and the content of composition could lead to the alleviation of these anxieties, and professional development opportunities, collaboratively planned and led, could help the entire program increase their (interactional) expertise with multimodal composition and writing studies generally. This would help all those working in the program understand what multimodality is and how multimodal composition can and should be integrated into FYC.

- The interviews revealed that the collaborative revision of the programmatic documents that articulate, outline, and define the curricular values of the program is a vital part of the process. Several directors mentioned the outcomes statement as one textual-rhetorical space wherein they made space for multimodal composition. If outcomes can make space for multimodal curricular transformation, then it would be useful for us to understand where the field is in terms of the language we use in our outcomes and what exactly that language (de)values.

This finding inspired Chapter 3, which explored what kinds of curricular content composition programs currently value and whether those values make space for or preclude multimodal composition. In that chapter, I examined over 1,000 outcomes from more than 80 programs working toward a panoramic understanding of the curricular values within composition programs. Unfortunately, outcomes that prescribe alphabetic writing dominated the corpus. Such outcomes, because they overdetermine the materials with/in which students compose, leave little space for multimodal composition and, consequently, multimodal curricular transformation. Just over half of the programs in the corpus included zero outcomes related to multimodal composition. However, there were useful takeaways for those interested in revising their outcomes to work toward multimodal curricular transformation. First, outcomes that focus on rhetorical knowledge and performance (including a knowledge of rhetorical terms, audience awareness, and focusing on a purpose, etc.) can make space for multimodal composition by requiring that students use *whatever is most effective for the task at hand* rather than defaulting to alphabetic writing. Rhetoric is a way for students to theorize the process of multimodal composing, and programs that want to include multimodality might return to and refocus on the position of rhetoric within the composition curriculum. Second, there are nuances that can be made to a program's current outcomes that can make space for multimodality by changing the vocabulary that we use to describe the work of the composition program (using text instead of essay, for example). These revisions can communicate to internal and external audiences that the content of composition includes more than just the alphabetic. Not least, presenting a capacious understanding of composition as multimodal rhetoric can help us work toward more equitable futures, operating against the racist and ableist impositions of SAE. Returning to and re-evaluating the language manifested within our outcomes with a focus on interrogating and challenging our values is part of the ongoing, intentional, reflective state of being that is multimodal curricular transformation. However, there are other programmatic documents that participate in the (re)making of our programs.

Chapter 4 turned to the assignments that we offer to students because those assignments instantiate and animate the values we articulate across documents and platforms. The assignment that emerged most frequently within the case studies was the remediation project. Remediation, as a literate practice, involves the reshaping of previously composed material for a new audience, medium, genre, and/or context. As an assignment within the composition curriculum, the remediation project requires that students engage rhetoric and multimodal composition. Remediation is not the only kind of multimodal project that can participate in multimodal curricular transformation, but the consistency with which it appeared in the case studies suggests that it might be the easiest to adopt because of the way it bridges the gap between alphabetic, academic writing (the content that gets reshaped in the act of remediation) and multimodal composition. It offers us a way to honor the history of composition programs while making space for and anticipating future curricular content. While some versions of the remediation project were more aligned with contemporary trends in writing studies scholarship than others, all of them remind us of the importance of rhetoric as a way to theorize the (multimodal) composing process, particularly the limitations and affordances of the materials with which we work. Additionally, the values manifested within these assignments are reinforced by a confluence of other programmatic documents: outcomes, mission statements, curricular descriptions, and other various venues made available to students and other stakeholders. Multimodal curricular transformation does involve assignments, but assignments alone cannot achieve transformation. It requires an ongoing commitment to rhetoric, to the full available means of persuasion, across documents and venues.

These data and findings suggest that multimodal curricular transformation can be initiated in various programmatic contexts. I offer the following heuristic—a guiding set of questions that emerge from these findings—as a way for programs to find their own way into transformation:

- What is multimodal curricular transformation?
- Why do you want to initiate or pursue multimodal curricular transformation?
- What are your program's values?
- How can you acknowledge, value, and strengthen the expertise of the faculty working within the program?
- How will multimodality be situated within the curriculum?
- What happens afterward?

In what follows, I will detail each question, how it connects to the findings I have presented in this book, and how it can help programs work toward multimodal curricular transformation.

What is multimodal curricular transformation?

The first question in the heuristic asks individuals to consider the definition of multimodal curricular transformation, which is absolutely necessary to make sure that all invested stakeholders understand the goal for which they are striving. As Chapter 2 demonstrated, multimodal composition can face resistance for various reasons, so it might be useful to begin the process with the following clarifications to establish common ground and ease possible anxieties:

- Multimodal curricular transformation *is not* the conflation of multimodality and digitality, and it does not mean that students must compose digital texts. As other scholars have noted, not all students have access to digital technologies, and not all students access digital technologies in the same way. Multimodal curricular transformation requires that students compose with more than alphabetic writing, engaging rhetorical composing strategies in multiple modes. To riff on the claim made by Jody Shipka (2013), multimodal curricular transformation includes, but is not limited to, the digital.
- Multimodal curricular transformation *is not* the addition of a low-stakes multimodal assignment at the end of the semester where students and instructors have little to invest in the project. Assignments like these imply that multimodal composition does not require as much time or effort as writing and only work to reinforce the privileged position of alphabetic writing in the academy. The program must acknowledge that multimodality is as rhetorically complex and rigorous as alphabetic writing and treat it accordingly.

- Multimodal curricular transformation *is not* an option for individual instructors to take up or not. Teaching faculty leave their positions for various reasons and take their pedagogical approaches with them when they go. To have an impact on the literacy practices of *all* students who move through the curriculum, multimodal composition must become an inextricable part of the entire program's curriculum, manifesting in both programmatic documents (outcomes, assignment sheets, guides, etc.), which communicate to internal and external audiences, and the practices that animate the curriculum.

- And not least, multimodal curricular transformation *is not* an abandonment of alphabetic writing. I am reluctant to address this misconception because I worry that, by making this point, I am giving credence to the racist, classist, and ableist assumptions regarding the perceived rigor of alphabetic writing, but I do believe it needs to be said: Multimodality does not do away with writing. Indeed, in reviewing scholarship and these case studies, we can see that students compose multimodally *in addition to and alongside* alphabetic writing in a transformed multimodal composition curriculum: the remediation project, for example, transforms previously composed academic writing (most typically a research project), and in addition to the remediation, students often compose rhetorical rationales and/or reflections. In this way, multimodal curricular transformation honors our past and allows us to move toward the future of (multimodal) composing.

Readers who are interested in beginning this process might share this information with their programs through conversation and discussion before offering this more thorough definition: multimodal curricular transformation is an ongoing programmatic commitment to allowing students the opportunity to cultivate their rhetorical fluency with the *full available means of persuasion*. This is the motivation for transformation, not a desire to have students compose with the latest digital technologies. Indeed, in *Remixing Composition* (2012), Jason Palmeri writes, "It is important to remember that our ultimate goal in the first-year course should not be to teach students to become professional 'new media' producers but rather to engage them in reflectively considering how theories of rhetoric and process can travel across modalities" (p. 153). In Chapter 2 the directors of the case study programs revealed that they wanted their students to be able to participate effectively and ethically in our global-digital world, and they wanted their programs to help their students cultivate the rhetorical agency necessary to do so. By shifting away from the hyper focus on alphabetic writing, by moving toward a curriculum that (re)emphasizes rhetoric, and by integrating multimodal composition within FYC curricula, multimodal curricular transformation simultaneously validates the literacies that students bring with them to our classrooms *and* positions us well to help students cultivate those literacies even further. I know this can be a significant programmatic shift. This kind of transformation asks us to reconsider the definition of FYC that we articulate in our documents and that we deliver to our students: Do we teach alphabetic writing (and writing only), or do we teach a capacious composition? This is, in essence, a cultural shift that asks us to move away from the way things have been done historically. The first, and perhaps most important, step in the process is sharing what multimodal curricular transformation is because it establishes the significant work ahead.

What are your program's values?

The next question maps out what I find to be the logical next step in multimodal curricular transformation: a discussion about programmatic, curricular, and individual values when it comes to composition. As I explored in Chapter 3, those values are reflected in the documents that constitute the program—outcomes statements, teachers' guides, assignment sheets, assessment rubrics, etc.—making space for or precluding certain kinds of curricular content. Programs that are interested in initiating multimodal curricular transformation should return to their documents and unpack the values that are at work therein. Outcomes, I have suggested in this book, might be one place to begin that process. In program-wide meetings, directors could ask if their program's current outcomes accurately reflect the values of the individuals currently working in the program. Do they reflect the disciplinary values of writing studies? Do they honor the literacy practices that students bring with them to our programs? If not, the program might consider new outcomes that will craft a more capacious version of composition to be delivered to students. I argued in Chapter 3 that those more capacious outcomes will embrace rhetoric as the foundation of composition, giving students access to the full available means of persuasion. That new vision of composition can and should be presented consistently across documents and platforms, reinforcing what it is that the program cares for, making implicit and explicit arguments to various stakeholders that alphabetic writing is only one part of the larger curriculum.

How can you acknowledge, value, and strengthen the expertise
of the faculty working within the program?

The directors I interviewed for Chapter 2 emphasized that the curricular revisions, particularly the revision of the program's documents, were the responsibility of the entire teaching faculty. This enacts Palmeri's recommendation that "this kind of curricular change can best be achieved through an evolutionary, flexible, and collaborative process in which instructors and program administrators work together to reinvent strategies for teaching multimodal composing within their own local contexts" (p. 153). Bringing in the teaching faculty to this process "recognizes that all teachers of writing have important insights to contribute to the development and enactment of multimodal pedagogies" (p. 154). For programs interested in making this move, it is important to realize that multimodal curricular transformation must be a collaborative enterprise, not only because collaboration is a useful and ethical feminist administrative practice, but because involving the teaching faculty in the process ensures the viability and sustainability of the curricular revisions. When I inquired about resistance to the changes, all of the directors mentioned that they did in fact face resistance, even within a collaborative, decentered administrative model. The way administrators negotiated that resistance was through feminist pragmatic rhetorical strategies. Rather than viewing resistance as unproductive or, frankly, infuriating, the directors utilized those moments as an opportunity to have open conversations with the faculty about their beliefs about writing and the pedagogical values that inform those beliefs. Approaching them collaboratively and inquiring about their personal pedagogical values would be a productive first step in achieving program-wide change. Additionally, this question can help administrators conceive of professional development opportunities that can be planned and scaffolded in such a way that they help everyone working in the program strengthen their familiarity with and expertise in writing studies. Collaboration, conversation, and the cultivation of expertise are all valuable and necessary parts of multimodal curricular transformation.

How will multimodality be situated within the curriculum?

In a transformed multimodal curriculum, multimodal assignments enact, enliven, and synthesize programmatic outcomes and disciplinary values, and they do so by requiring students to engage rhetoric. Administrators and teaching faculty who wish to move their programs toward multimodal curricular transformation will need to determine exactly how multimodality will be situated in their local curricula. In the case study programs that I analyzed, the most common assignment was the remediation project. These kinds of projects are an act of rhetorical reframing and reshaping, in which students transform work they have done in a previous project. Most often, this appears as a continuation of a research paper—students take the research they have conducted and share that with a different audience using modes and media not available to them in a traditional alphabetic writing assignment. Thus, while the research paper is still entrenched within FYC curricula, its entrenchment means that composition programs already have a way into multimodal curricular transformation. Including a remediation project after the major research paper, perhaps by requiring that students share their research with a nonacademic audience, would help programs align themselves with the case studies I have presented here and, correspondingly, with the current trends in writing studies scholarship. This finding mirrors another of Palmeri's recommendations, which is that it

> is reasonable for writing program administrators and faculty to begin transforming curricula to include *one formal assignment sequence* in which students attempt to "translate" an argument from one modality to another. . . . As students engage in the process of attempting to translate an argument from one modality to another, we can ask them to reflect critically about the unique affordances and limitations of various forms of composing—preparing them to make informed rhetorical choices about which modalities will best enable them to convey their persuasive arguments. (pp. 152–153, emphasis added)

This is just one possibility, though. I have some reservations about the remediation project as it currently exists, particularly because it requires that alphabetic writing (the research paper) *precede* multimodal composition. As I mentioned in Chapter 4, this could, in effect, suggest that alphabetic writing is more rigorous or serious than multimodal composing. A different manifestation could ask students to present their research multimodally first and then compose a more traditional alphabetic essay afterward. After this, students might compose a (multimodal) reflective piece wherein they consider the sequencing of the projects and what they learned about both multimodal and alphabetic composing in the process. In doing so, students would engage in a different kind of dialectic, gaining a deeper appreciation for one way of making meaning by examining it alongside the other. Exactly how multimodality manifests within the curriculum is less important than the fact that it does take on a central position, and those who wish to engage in the process of multimodal curricular transformation will want to discern what that position will be for their own programs through collaborative consensus-making with their teaching faculty.

And what happens afterward?

Curricular changes should not be implemented and then abandoned. In fact, as E. Shelley Reid (2003) has argued, it is perhaps more productive for programs to perceive themselves as within a constant state of *changing*, which "may benefit teachers, administrators, and programs as a whole by encouraging the kind of reflective practice that we see as central to scholarship and practice in composition" (p. 11). By entering this state of reflective practice qua changing, Reid argues, programs position themselves to be more adaptive and responsive to both disciplinary advances and student needs. Thus, it is important that those who engage in the process of multimodal curricular transformation remember that it is *not an endpoint* to achieve but rather a state of being in which they might exist, constantly finding new and deeper ways to engage rhetoric and foster multimodal composition. The case studies that I present in this book suggest that professional development meetings might be a way to keep the culture of the program in this state. These meetings could do the following:

- Define and redefine rhetoric and the role of rhetorical concepts in the composing process;
- Share contemporary research and theories with instructional faculty, especially for programs that are staffed by those without terminal degrees in writing studies, to strengthen their familiarity with multimodal composition and cultivate their interactional expertise;
- Provide examples of both assignments that invite/require/foster multimodal composition *and* successful examples of those assignments created by students from within the program;
- Offer moments for the teaching faculty to share their concerns or anxieties about any changes proposed by the program; and
- Discuss ways to respond to and assess multimodal projects.

Programmatic cultures are an accumulation of texts and practices. If the documents of the program have been collaboratively revised to center rhetoric and multimodal composing (as the previous questions in this heuristic recommended), then it follows logically that professional development would be a productive practice that programs could use to maintain the cultural shift that multimodal curricular transformation strives for.

I offer this heuristic with the wholehearted belief that multimodal curricular transformation, while currently uncommon at the national level, is quite achievable if readers utilize the data-driven strategies that I have offered in this conclusion. The programs that I examined for the purposes of this book do good work, but they are not unique. The directors that I interviewed were skillful and knowledgeable administrators (who were exceptionally generous with their time), but they operated within a set of constraints in which most composition directors find themselves. At the intersection of (feminist) programmatic practices and strategies, a commitment to the full available rhetorical means and a desire to review and rearticulate values in public-facing and internal documents, these directors brought their programs into multimodal curricular transformation. This work is so very necessary for the vitality of composition programs. Through a commitment to multimodal composition, we can make space for emerging literacy practices, new forms of texts, and the rhetorical processes associated with both. Through multimodal curricular transformation, we return to and reinvigorate our connection to the history of rhetoric and how it contours human (inter)actions. And thus, through multimodal curricular transformation, we position ourselves as educators who can help the people who move through our classrooms and programs cultivate the knowledge necessary to cross contexts, to speak to multiple audiences, to use the available means flexibly and adroitly, and to effect change in their private and public lives.

REFERENCES

Adler-Kassner, L. (2008). *The activist WPA: Changing stories about writing and writers*. Utah State University Press.

Adsanatham, C., Alexander, P., Carsey, K., Dubisar, A., Fedeczo, W., Landrum, D., Lewiecki-Wilson, C., McKee, H., Moore, K., Patterson, G., & Polak, M. (2013). Going multimodal: Programmatic, curricular, and programmatic change. In T. Bowen & C. Whithaus (Eds.), *Multimodal literacies and emerging genres* (pp. 283–312). University of Pittsburgh Press.

Alexander, J., & Rhodes, J. (2014). *On multimodality: New media in composition studies*. CCCC/NCTE.

Alexander, K. P., DePalma, M., & Ringer, J. M. (2016). Adaptive remediation and the facilitation of transfer in multiliteracy center contexts. *Computers and Composition, 41*, 32–45.

Alvarez, S. (2016). Taco literacies: ethnography, foodways, and emotions through Mexican food writing. *Composition Forum, 34*.

Angay-Crowder, T., Choi, J., & Yi, Y. (2013). Putting multiliteracies into practice: Digital storytelling for multilingual adolescents in a summer program. *TESL Canada Journal, 30*(2), 36–45.

Atwill, J. M. (1998). *Rhetoric reclaimed: Aristotle and the liberal arts tradition*. Cornell University Press.

Ball, C. E., & Charlton, C. (2015). All writing is multimodal. In L. Adler-Kassner & E. Wardle (Eds.), *Naming what we know: Threshold concepts of writing studies* (pp. 42–43). Utah State University Press.

Banks, A. (2015). 2015 CCCC chair's address: Ain't no walls behind the sky, baby. Funk, flight, freedom. *College Composition and Communication, 67*(2), 267–279.

Bawarshi, A. S., & Reiff, M. J. (2010). *Genre: An introduction to history, theory, research, and pedagogy*. Parlor Press.

Bearden, L. (2019a). Favorable outcomes: How outcomes can make space for multimodal curricula. *WPA: Writing Program Administration, 43*(1), 139–160.

Bearden, L. (2019b). Transformative programs, transformed practice: Multiliteracies and the work of the composition program. *Journal of College Literacy and Learning, 45*, 69–81.

Bishop, W. (2002). Steal this assignment: The radical revision. In C. Moore & P. O'Neill (Eds.), *Practice in context* (pp. 205–222). CCCC/NCTE.

Blankenship, L. (2019). *Changing the subject: A theory of rhetorical empathy*. Utah State University Press.

Bolter, J. D., & Grusin, R. (1999). *Remediation: Understanding new media*. MIT Press.

Brady, L. (2006). A greenhouse for writing program change. *WPA: Writing Program Administration, 29*(3), 27–43.

Brewer, M. (2020). *Conceptions of literacy: Graduate instructors and the teaching of first-year composition*. Utah State University Press.

Brice, C. (2005). Coding data in qualitative research on L2 writing: Issues and complications. In P. K. Matsuda & T. Silva (Eds.), *Second language writing research: Perspectives on the process of knowledge construction*. Routledge.

Callaway, M. (2013). The WPA learning outcomes: What role should technology play? In N. N. Behm, G. R. Glau, D. H. Holdstein, D. Roen, & E. M. White (Eds.), *The WPA outcomes statement: A decade later* (pp. 271–284). Parlor Press.

https://doi.org/10.7330/9781646422135.c006

Ceraso, S. (2014). (Re)Educating the senses: Multimodal listening, bodily learning, and the composition of sonic experiences. *College English, 77*(2), 102–123.

Ceraso, S. (2018). *Multimodal pedagogies for embodied listening.* University of Pittsburgh Press.

Conference on College Composition and Communication. (2014). *Students' right to their own language (with bibliography).* https://cccc.ncte.org/cccc/resources/positions/srtol summary

Conference on College Composition and Communication. (2020). *This ain't another statement! This is a DEMAND for Black Linguistic Justice.* https://cccc.ncte.org/cccc/demand -for-black-linguistic-justice

Connors, R. J. (1997). *Composition-rhetoric: Backgrounds, theory, and pedagogy.* University of Pittsburgh Press.

Cope, B., & Kalantzis, M. (2000). *Multiliteracies: Literacy learning and the design of social futures.* Routledge.

Cope, B., & Kalantzis, M. (2009). "Multiliteracies": New literacies, new learning. *Pedagogies: An International Journal, 4*(3), 164–195.

Corbin, J., & Strauss, A. (2008). *Basics of qualitative research: Techniques and procedures for developing grounded theory.* Sage.

Council of Writing Program Administrators. (2014, July 17). *WPA outcomes statement for first-year composition (3.0).* http://wpacouncil.org/positions/outcomes.html

DePalma, M. (2015). Tracing transfer across media: Investigating writers' perceptions of cross-contextual and rhetorical reshaping in processes of remediation. *College Composition and Communication, 66*(4), 615–642.

Devitt, A. J. (1993). Generalizing about genre: New conceptions of an old concept. *College Composition and Communication, 44*(4), 573–586.

Dobrin, S. I. (2011). *Postcomposition.* Southern Illinois University Press.

Downs, D., & Wardle, E. (2007). Teaching about writing, righting misconceptions: (Re)Envisioning "first-year composition" as "introduction to writing studies." *College Composition and Communication, 58*(4), 552–584.

Dryer, D. B. (2012). At a mirror, darkly: The imagined undergraduate writers of ten novice composition instructors. *College Composition and Communication, 63*(3), 420–452.

Dryer, D., Bowden, D., Brunk-Chavez, B. L., Harrington, S., Halbritter, B., & Yancey, K. B. (2014). Revising outcomes for a multimodal, digitally composed world: The WPA outcomes statement for first-year composition 3.0. *WPA: Writing Program Administration, 38*(1), 129–143.

Dunn, J. S., Fabian, S., Gray, S., Pavlock, K. C., Levit-Phillips, H., Soebbing, S., Estrem, H., & Adler-Kassner, L. (2013). In N. N. Behm, G. R. Glau, D. H. Holdstein, D. Roen, & E. M. White (Eds.), *The WPA outcomes statement: A decade later* (pp. 209–229). Parlor Press.

Dyson, A. H, & Genishi, C. (2005). *On the case: Approaches to language and literacy research.* Teachers College Press.

Ebest, S. B. (2005). *Changing the way we teach: Writing and resistance in the training of teaching assistants.* Southern Illinois University Press.

Ferruci, S., & DeRosa, S. (2019). Multimodality, transfer, and rhetorical awareness: Analyzing the choices of undergraduate writers. In J. C. Lee & S. Khadka (Eds.), *Bridging the multimodal gap: From theory to practice* (pp. 201–224). Utah State University Press.

Fitzpatrick, K. (2011). *Planned obsolescence: Publishing, technology, and the future of the academy.* New York University Press.

Fordham, T., & Oakes, H. (2013). Rhetoric across modes, rhetoric across campus: Faculty and students building a multimodal curriculum. In T. Bowen & C. Whithaus (Eds.), *Multimodal literacies and emerging genres in student compositions* (pp. 313–335). University of Pittsburgh Press.

Foss, S. K., & Griffin, C. L. (1995). Beyond persuasion: A proposal for an invitational rhetoric. *Communications Monographs, 62*(1), 2–18.

Gearhart, S. (1979). The womanization of rhetoric. *Women's Studies International Quarterly*, 2(2), 195–201.

George, D. (2002). From analysis to design: visual communication in the teaching of writing. *College Composition and Communication*, 54(1), 11–39.

Giberson, G., & Moriarty, T. A. (2010). *What we are becoming: Developments in undergraduate writing majors.* Utah State University Press.

Giltrow, J. (2002). Meta-genre. In R. Coe, L. Lindgard, & T. Teslenko (Eds.), *The rhetoric and ideology of genre* (pp. 187–205). Hampton Press.

Goodburn, A., & Leverenz, C. S. (1998). Feminist writing program administration: Resisting the bureaucrat within. In S. C. Jarratt & L. Worsham (Eds.), *Feminism and composition studies: In other words* (pp. 276–290). MLA.

Graban, T. S., Charlton, C., & Charlton, J. (2013). Multivalent composition and the reinvention of expertise. In T. Bowen & C. Whithaus (Eds.), *Multimodal literacies and emerging genres in student compositions* (pp. 248–281). University of Pittsburgh Press.

Graban, T. S., & Ryan, K. J. (2005). From "what is" to "what is possible": Theorizing curricular document revision as in(ter)vention and reform. *WPA: Writing Program Administration*, 28(3), 89–112.

Grabill, J. T., & Blythe, S. (2010). Citizens doing science in public spaces: Rhetorical invention, semiotic remediation, and simple little texts. In P. A. Prior & J. A. Hengst (Eds.), *Exploring semiotic remediation as discourse practice* (pp. 184–205). Palgrave Macmillan.

Gresham, M. (2013). Ripple effect: Adopting and adapting the WPA outcomes. In N. N. Behm, G. R. Glau, D. H. Holdstein, D. Roen, & E. M. White (Eds.), *The WPA outcomes statement: A decade later* (pp. 179–190). Parlor Press.

Grettano, T., Ingalls, R., & Morse, T. A. (2013). The perilous vision of the outcomes statement. In N. N. Behm, G. R. Glau, D. H. Holdstein, D. Roen, & E. M. White (Eds.), *The WPA outcomes statement: A decade later* (pp. 45–57). Parlor Press.

Grouling, J. (2015). Resistance and identity formation: The journey of the graduate student-teacher. *Composition Forum*, 32.

Gunner, J. (2002). Collaborative administration. In S. C. Brown & T. Enos (Eds.), *The writing program administrator's resource: A guide to reflective institutional practice* (pp. 253–262). Lawrence Erlbaum.

Handa, C. (2004). *Visual rhetoric in a digital world: A critical sourcebook.* Bedford/St. Martin's.

Halbritter, B. (2013). *Mics, cameras, symbolic action: Audio-visual rhetoric for writing teachers.* Parlor Press.

Hansen, K. (2018). Discipline and profession: Can the field of rhetoric and writing be both? In R. Malencyzk, S. Miller-Cochran, E. Wardle, & K. B. Yancey (Eds.), *Composition, rhetoric, and disciplinarity* (pp. 134–158). Utah State University Press.

Harrison, K. (2013). Building a writing program with the WPA outcomes: Authority, ethos, and professional identity. In N. N. Behm, G. R. Glau, D. H. Holdstein, D. Roen, & E. M. White (Eds.), *The WPA outcomes statement: A decade later* (pp. 32–44). Parlor Press.

Haworth, J. G., & Conrad, C. F. (1990). Curricular transformations: traditional and emerging voices in the academy. In J. G. Haworth & C. F. Conrad (Eds.), *Curriculum in transition: Perspectives on the undergraduate experience* (pp. 3–19). Simon and Schuster.

Hedges, E. (1996). Curriculum transformation: A brief overview. *Women's Studies Quarterly*, 24(3/4), 16–22.

Hein, S. G., & Riegel, C. D. (2011). A systematic model for program evaluation and curricular transformation: A tale from the trenches. *International CHRIE Conference-Refereed Track*, 11.

Hill, C. & Ericsson, P. F. (2014). The crystal ball project: Predicting the future of composition and the preparation of composition instructors. *The Clearing House: A Journal of Educational Strategies, Issues, and Ideas*, 87(4), 143–148.

Hocks, M. (2003). Understanding visual rhetoric in digital writing environments. *College Composition and Communication*, 54(4), 629–656.

Hokanson, R. O. (2005). Using writing outcomes to enhance teaching and learning: Averno College's experience. In S. Harrington, K. Rhodes, R. O. Fischer, & R. Malenczyk (Eds.), *The outcomes book: Debate and consensus after the WPA outcomes statement* (pp. 150–161). Utah State U P.

Horn, R. A. (2002). *Understanding educational reform: A reference handbook.* ABC-CLIO, Inc.

Horner, B., Lu, M. Z., Royster, J. J., & Trimbur, J. (2011). Language difference in writing: Toward a translingual approach. *College English, 73*(3), 303-321.

Inoue, A. (2015). *Antiracist writing assessment ecologies: Teaching and assessing writing for a socially just future.* Parlor Press.

Irvin, L. L. (2009). The activist WPA in action: A profile of the first-year writing program at Eastern Michigan University. *Composition Forum, 20.*

Isaacs, E. J. (2018). *Writing at the state U: Instruction and administration at 106 comprehensive universities.* Utah State University Press.

Isaacs, E., & Knight, M. (2013). Assessing the impact of the outcomes statement. In N. N. Behm, G. R. Glau, D. H. Holdstein, D. Roen, & E. M. White (Eds.), *The WPA outcomes statement: A decade later* (pp. 285–383). Parlor Press.

Jacobsen, C., Miller-Cochran, S., & Rodrigo, S. (2013). The WPA outcomes statement and disciplinary authority. In N. N. Behm, G. R. Glau, D. H. Holdstein, D. Roen, & E. M. White (Eds.), *The WPA outcomes statement: A decade later* (pp. 107–123). Parlor Press.

Khadka, S., & Lee, J. C. (2019). *Bridging the multimodal gap: From theory to practice.* Utah State University Press.

Khalil, S. M. (2013). From resistance to acceptance and use of technology in academia. *Open Praxis, 5*(2), 151-163.

Kress, G. (2005). Gains and losses: New forms of texts, knowledge, and learning. *Computers and Composition, 22*(1), 5-22.

Kress, G. (2010). *Multimodality: A social semiotic approach to contemporary communication.* Routledge.

Kynard, C. (2007). "Wanted: Some black long distance [writers]": Blackboard Flava-flavin and other afrodigital experiences in the classroom. *Computers and Composition, 24*(1), 329-345.

Lee, J. C., & Khadka, S. (2018). *Designing and implementing multimodal curricula and programs.* Routledge.

Lee, R. (2018). Surveying the available modes of persuasion. In J. C. Lee & S. Khadka (Eds.), *Designing and implementing multimodal curricula and programs* (pp. 89–110). Routledge.

Lerner, N. (2005). The teacher-student writing conference and the desire for intimacy. *College English, 68*(2), 186-208.

Leverenz, C. S. (2010). What's ethics got to do with it? Feminist ethics and administrative work in rhetoric and composition. In K. Ratcliffe & R. Rickly (Eds.), *Performing feminism and administration in rhetoric and composition studies* (pp. 3–18). Hampton Press.

Leverenz, C. S. (2014). Design thinking and the wicked problem of teaching writing. *Computers and Composition, 33,* 1–12.

Leverenz, C. S. (2016). Redesigning writing outcomes. *WPA: Writing Program Administration, 40*(1), 33–49.

Linneberg, M. S., & Korsgaard, S. (2019). Coding qualitative data: A synthesis guiding the novice. *Qualitative Research Journal, 19*(3), 259-270.

Maid, B. M., & D'Angelo, B. J. (2013). Is rhetorical knowledge the uber-outcome? In N. N. Behm, G. R. Glau, D. H. Holdstein, D. Roen, & E. M. White (Eds.), *The WPA outcomes statement: A decade later* (pp. 257-270). Parlor Press.

Martin, C. S., Hirsu, L., Gonzales, L., & Alvarez, S. P. (2019). Pedagogies of digital composing through a translingual approach. *Computers and Composition, 52,* 142–157.

McClure, J. L. (2005). The outcomes statement at a community college: Verification, accreditation, and articulation. In S. Harrington, K. Rhodes, R. O. Fischer, & R.

Malenczyk (Eds.), *The outcomes book: Debate and consensus after the WPA outcomes statement* (pp. 51–59). Utah State University Press.

McKee, H. (2006). Sound matters: Notes toward the analysis and design of sound in multimodal webtexts. *Computers and Composition, 23*(3), 335–354.

McLeod, S. H. (2007). *Writing program administration.* Parlor Press.

Melzer, D. (2014). *Writing across the curriculum: A national study of college writing.* Utah State University Press.

Merriam, S. B. (2009). *Qualitative research: A guide to design and implementation.* Jossey-Bass.

Miller, C. R. (1984). Genre as social action. *Quarterly Journal of Speech, 70*(2), 151–167.

Mills, K. A. (2008). Transformed practice in a pedagogy of multiliteracies. *Pedagogies: An International Journal, 3*(2), 109–128.

Moerschell, L. (2009). Resistance to technological change in academia. *Current Issues in Education, 11*(6). 1–9.

National Census of Writing. (2013). https://writingcensus.swarthmore.edu/

National Council of Teachers of English. (2005). *NCTE position statement on multimodal literacies.* http://www.ncte.org/positions/statements/multimodalliteracies

Olson, W. (2013). The politics of pedagogy: The outcomes statement and basic writing. In N. N. Behm, G. R. Glau, D. H. Holdstein, D. Roen, & E. M. White (Eds.), *The WPA outcomes statement: A decade later* (pp. 18–31). Parlor Press.

Oreg, S. (2006). Personality, context, and resistance to organizational change. *European Journal of Work and Organizational Psychology, 15*(1), 73–101.

Palmeri, J. (2012). *Remixing composition: A history of multimodal writing pedagogy.* Southern Illinois University Press.

Perryman-Clark, S. (2016). Who we are(n't) assessing: Racializing language and writing assessment in writing program administration. *College English, 79*(2), 206–211.

Pettipiece, D., & Everett, J. (2013). Ethos and topoi: Using the outcomes statement rhetorically to achieve the centrality and autonomy of writing programs. In N. N. Behm, G. R. Glau, D. H. Holdstein, D. Roen, & E. M. White (Eds.), *The WPA outcomes statement: A decade later* (pp. 191–208). Parlor Press.

Porter, J. E. (2009). Sustaining a research center: Building the research and outreach profile for a writing program. In D. N. DeVoss, H. A. McKee, & R. Selfe (Eds.), *Technological ecologies and sustainability.* Computers and Composition Digital Press. http://ccdigitalpress.org/tes/

Powell, P. R. (2020). *Writing changes: Alphabetic text and multimodal composition.* The Modern Language Association of America.

Prior, P. (2009). From speech genres to mediated multimodal genre systems: Bakhtin, Voloshinov, and the question of writing. In C. Bazerman, A. Bonini, & D. Figueredo (Eds.), *Genre in a changing world* (pp. 17–34). WAC Clearinghouse.

Prior, P., & Hengst, J. (2010). *Exploring semiotic remediation as discourse practice.* Palgrave Macmillan.

Prior, P., Solberg, J., Berry, P., Bellwoar, H., Chewning, B., Lunsford, K. J., Rohan, L., Roozen, K., Sheridan-Rabideau, M. P., Shipka, J., Ittersum, D. V., & Walker, J. (2007). Re-situating and re-mediating the canons: A cultural-historical remapping of rhetorical activity. *Kairos, 11*(3).

Purdy, J. P. (2014). What can design thinking offer writing studies? *College Composition and Communication, 65*(4), 612–641.

Reid, E. S. (2003). A changing for the better: Curriculum revision as reflective practice in teaching and administration. *WPA: Writing Program Administration, 26*(3), 10–27.

Reiff, M. J., Bawarshi, A. S., Ballif, M., & Weisser, C. (2015). *Ecologies of writing programs: Program profiles in context.* Parlor Press.

Rìos, G. (2015). Cultivating land-based literacies and rhetorics. *Literacy in Composition Studies, 3*(1), 60–70.

Rhodes, K., Peckham, I., Bergmann, L. S., & Condon, W. (2005). The outcomes project: The insiders' history. In S. Harrington, K. Rhodes, R. O. Fischer, & R. Malenczyk (Eds.), *The outcomes book: Debate and consensus after the WPA outcomes statement* (pp. 8–17). Utah State University Press.

Ryan, K. J., & Graban, T. S. (2009). Theorizing feminist pragmatic rhetoric as a communicative act for the composition practicum. *College Composition and Communication, 61*(1), W277–W299.

Schiavone, A. (2017). Consumption, production, and rhetorical knowledge in visual in multimodal textbooks. *College English, 74*(4), 358–380.

Seidman, I. (2006). *Interviewing as qualitative research: A guide for researchers in education and the social sciences.* Teachers College Press.

Selfe, C. L. (1999). Technology and literacy: A short story about the perils of not paying attention. *College Composition and Communication, 50*(3), 411–436.

Selfe, C. L., & Ericsson, P. F. (2005). Expanding our understanding of composing outcomes. In S. Harrington, K. Rhodes, R. O. Fischer, & R. Malenczyk (Eds.), *The outcomes book: Debate and consensus after the WPA outcomes statement* (pp. 32–38). Utah State University Press.

Selfe, R. J., & Selfe, C. L. (2008). "Convince me!" Valuing multimodal literacies and composing public service announcements. *Theory into Practice, 47*(2), 83–92.

Selfe, R. J. (2005). *Sustainable computer environments: Cultures of support in English studies and language arts.* Hampton Press.

Sheppard, J. (2009). The rhetorical work of multimedia production practices: It's more than just technical skill. *Computers and Composition, 26*(2), 122–131.

Sheridan, D. M., Ridolfo, J., & Michel, A. J. (2012). *The available means of persuasion: Mapping a theory and pedagogy of multimodal public rhetoric.* Parlor Press.

Shipka, J. (2005). A multimodal task-based framework for composing. *College Composition and Communication, 57*(2), 277–306.

Shipka, J. (2011). *Toward a composition made whole.* University of Pittsburgh Press.

Shipka, J. (2013). Including, but not limited to, the digital: Composing multimodal texts. In T. Bowen & C. Whithaus (Eds.), *Multimodal literacies and emerging genres in student compositions* (pp.73–89). University of Pittsburgh Press.

Sidler, M., Smith, E. O., & Morris, R. (Eds.). (2008). *Computers in the composition classroom: A critical sourcebook.* Bedford/St. Martin's.

Siegel Finer, B., & White-Farnham, J. (2017). *Writing program architecture: Thirty cases for reference and research.* Utah State University Press.

Smagorinsky, P. (2008). The methods section as conceptual epicenter in construction social science research reports. *Written Communication, 25*(3), 389–411.

Smitherman, G. (1999). CCCC's role in the struggle for language rights. *College Composition and Communication, 50*(3), 349–376.

Sommers, J. (2014). Revisiting radical revision. In T. Roeder and R. Gatto (Eds.), *Critical expressivism: Theory and practice in the composition classroom* (pp. 289–304). The WAC Clearinghouse and Parlor Press.

Strickland, D. (2011). *The managerial unconscious in the history of composition studies.* Southern Illinois University Press.

Stroupe, C. (2000). Visualizing English: Recognizing the hybrid literacy of visual and verbal authorship on the web. *College English, 62*(5), 607–632.

VanKooten, C. (2016). Identifying components of meta-awareness about composition: Toward a theory and methodology for writing studies. *Composition Forum, 33.*

VanKooten, C., & A. Berkley, A. (2016). Messy problem-exploring through video in first-year composition: Assessing what counts. *Computers and Composition, 40,* 151–163.

Walker, J. R. (2007). Constructing a BIG text: Developing a multimodal master plan for composition instruction. In Prior, P., Solberg, J., Berry, P., Bellwoar, H., Chewning, B., Lunsford, K. J., Rohan, L., Roozen, K., Sheridan-Rabideau, M. P., Shipka, J., Van Ittersum, D., & Walker, J. (Eds.), *Re-situating and remediating the canons: A cultural-historical remapping of rhetorical activity. Kairos, 11*(3).

Wardle, E. (2012). Creative repurposing for expansive learning: Considering "problem-exploring" and "answer-getting" dispositions in individuals and fields. *Composition Forum, 26*(1).

Wardle, E., & Scott, J. B. (2015). Defining and developing expertise in a writing and rhetoric department. *WPA: Writing Program Administration, 39*(1), 72–93.

White, E. M. (1991). Use it or lose it: Power and the WPA. *WPA: Writing Program Administration, 15*(1–2), 3–12.

White, E. M. (2005). The origins of the outcomes statement. In S. Harrington, K. Rhodes, R. O. Fischer, & R. Malenczyk (Eds.), *The outcomes book: Debate and consensus after the WPA outcomes statement* (pp. 3–7). Utah State University Press.

Whithaus, C. (2005). *Teaching and evaluating writing in the age of computers and high-stakes testing.* Routledge.

Wilhoit, S. (2005). The WPA outcomes statement goes to high school. In S. Harrington, K. Rhodes, R. O. Fischer, & R. Malenczyk (Eds.), *The outcomes book: Debate and consensus after the WPA outcomes statement* (pp. 39–50). Utah State University Press.

Wysocki, A. F. (2005). awaywithwords: On the possibilities in unavailable designs. *Computers and Composition, 22*(1), 55–62.

Yancey, K. B. (1998). *Reflection in the writing classroom.* Utah State University Press.

Yancey, K. B. (2001). Digitized student portfolios. In B. L. Cambridge, S. Kahn, D. P. Tompkins, & K. B. Yancey (Eds.), *Electronic portfolios: Emerging practices in student, faculty, and institutional learning* (pp. 15–30). Stylus.

Yancey, K. B. (2004a). Made not only in words: Composition in a new key. *College Composition and Communication, 56*(2), 297–328.

Yancey, K. B. (2004b). Postmodernism, palimpsest, and portfolios: Theoretical issues in the representation of student work. *College Composition and Communication, 55*(4), 738–761.

Yancey, K. B. (2012). Writing assessment in the early twenty-first century: A primer. In K. Ritter & P. K. Matsuda (Eds.), *Exploring composition studies: Sites, issues, & perspectives* (pp. 167–187). Utah State University Press.

Yancey, K. B. (2016). *A rhetoric of reflection.* Utah State University Press.

Yancey, K. B, Robertson, L., & Taczak, K. (2014). *Writing across contexts: Transfer, composition, and sites of writing.* Utah State University Press.

Yergeau, M. R., Brewer, E., Kerschbaum, S., Oswal, S., Price, M., Selfe, C. L., Salvo, M. J., & Howes, F. (2013). Multimodality in motion: Disability & kairotic spaces. *Kairos, 18*(1).

INDEX

ABOUT THE AUTHOR

Dr. Logan Bearden directs the First-Year Writing Program and Digital Studio at Eastern Michigan University. He teaches courses in rhetoric, writing, media studies, and the teaching of writing at the undergraduate and graduate level. He has published on outcomes statements, multimodal composition, and writing program administration in various venues. His co-edited collection, *Radiant Figures: Visual Rhetorics in Everyday Administrative Contexts* (with Derek Mueller and Rachel Gramer), is available through Computers and Composition Digital Press.